The Congo and the
Cameroons

Mount Cameroon, 1894

MARY KINGSLEY

The Congo and the Cameroons

GREAT
JOURNEYS

TED SMART

PENGUIN BOOKS

Published by the Penguin Group
Penguin Books Ltd, 80 Strand, London WC2R ORL, England
Penguin Group (USA) Inc., 375 Hudson Street, New York, New York 10014, USA
Penguin Group (Canada), 90 Eglinton Avenue East, Suite 700, Toronto, Ontario, Canada M4P 2Y3
(a division of Pearson Penguin Canada Inc.)
Penguin Ireland, 25 St Stephen's Green, Dublin 2, Ireland (a division of Penguin Books Ltd)
Penguin Group (Australia), 250 Camberwell Road, Camberwell, Victoria 3124, Australia
(a division of Pearson Australia Group Pty Ltd)
Penguin Books India Pvt Ltd, 11 Community Centre, Panchsheel Park, New Delhi – 110 017, India
Penguin Group (NZ), 67 Apollo Drive, Rosedale, North Shore 0632, New Zealand
(a division of Pearson New Zealand Ltd)
Penguin Books (South Africa) (Pty) Ltd, 24 Sturdee Avenue, Rosebank, Johannesburg 2196, South Africa

Penguin Books Ltd, Registered Offices: 80 Strand, London WC2R ORL, England

www.penguin.com

Travels in West Africa first published in 1897
This extract published in Penguin Books 2007

3

All rights reserved

Inside-cover maps by Jeff Edwards

Typeset by Rowland Phototypesetting Ltd, Bury St Edmunds, Suffolk
Printed in England by Clays Ltd, St Ives plc

ISBN 978-0-141-02551-3

This edition produced for The Book People Ltd,
Hall Wood Avenue, Haydock, St. Helens, WA11 9UL

Contents

The remarkable Mary Kingsley (1862–1900) made three journeys to Africa. In the first two journeys she roamed around West and Equatorial West Africa, from Sierra Leone to Angola, the second journey being particularly memorable for her travels through the rivers and forests of modern Gabon and her ascent of Mount Cameroon, then in the German colony of Kamerun. She developed through her experiences both an overwhelming enthusiasm for Africa and a matching scepticism about European imperialism and missionary work. It was on her return from the second African journey that she wrote her bestselling *Travels in West Africa* (1897). Her third and final journey to Africa resulted in her death, aged thirty-seven, from enteric fever while working as a volunteer nurse in a hospital for Afrikaner POWs during the Boer War.

Mangrove Swamps and Crocodiles

There is a uniformity in the habits of West Coast rivers, from the Volta to the Coanza, which is, when you get used to it, very taking. Excepting the Congo, the really great river comes out to sea with as much mystery as possible; lounging lazily along among its mangrove swamps in a what's-it-matter-when-one-comes-out and where's-the-hurry style, through quantities of channels inter-communicating with each other. Each channel, at first sight as like the other as peas in a pod, is bordered on either side by green-black walls of mangroves, which Captain Lugard graphically described as seeming 'as if they had lost all count of the vegetable proprieties, and were standing on stilts with their branches tucked up out of the wet, leaving their gaunt roots exposed in mid-air.' High-tide or low-tide, there is little difference in the water; the river, be it broad or narrow, deep or shallow, looks like a pathway of polished metal; for it is as heavy weighted with stinking mud as water e'er can be, ebb or flow, year out and year in. But the difference in the banks, though an unending alternation between two appearances, is weird.

At high-water you do not see the mangroves

displaying their ankles in the way that shocked Captain Lugard. They look most respectable, their foliage rising densely in a wall irregularly striped here and there by the white line of an aërial root, coming straight down into the water from some upper branch as straight as a plummet, in the strange, knowing way an aërial root of a mangrove does, keeping the hard straight line until it gets some two feet above water-level, and then spreading out into blunt fingers with which to dip into the water and grasp the mud. Banks indeed at high water can hardly be said to exist, the water stretching away into the mangrove swamps for miles and miles, and you can then go, in a suitable small canoe, away among these swamps as far as you please.

This is a fascinating pursuit. For people who like that sort of thing it is just the sort of thing they like, as the art critic of a provincial town wisely observed anent an impressionist picture recently acquired for the municipal gallery. But it is a pleasure to be indulged in with caution; for one thing, you are certain to come across crocodiles. Now a crocodile drifting down in deep water, or lying asleep with its jaws open on a sand-bank in the sun, is a picturesque adornment to the landscape when you are on the deck of a steamer, and you can write home about it and frighten your relations on your behalf; but when you are away among the swamps in a small dug-out canoe, and that crocodile and his relations are awake – a thing he makes a point of being at flood tide because of fish coming along – and when he has got his foot upon his native heath – that is to say, his tail within holding reach of his native mud – he is highly interesting, and you may not be able to write home about him – and you get frightened on your own behalf. For crocodiles can, and often do, in such places, grab at people in small canoes. I have known of several natives losing their lives in this way; some native villages are approachable from the main river by a short cut, as it were, through the mangrove swamps, and the inhabitants of such villages will now and then go across this way with small canoes instead of by the constant channel to the village, which is almost always winding. In addition to this un-pleasantness you are liable – until you realise the danger from experience, or have native advice on the point – to get tide-trapped away in the swamps, the water falling round you when you are away in some deep pool or lagoon, and you find you cannot get back to the main river. For you cannot get out and drag your canoe across the stretches of mud that separate you from it, because the mud is of too unstable a nature and too deep, and sinking into it means staying in it, at any rate until some geologist of the remote future may come across you, in a fossilised state, when that mangrove swamp shall have become dry land. Of course if you really want a truly safe investment in Fame, and really care about Posterity, and Posterity's Science, you will jump over into the black batter-like, stinking slime, cheered by the thought of the terrific sensation you will produce 20,000 years hence, and the care you will be taken of then by your fellow-creatures, in a museum. But if you are a mere ordinary person of a retiring nature, like me, you stop in your lagoon until the tide rises again; most of your attention is directed to dealing with an 'at home' to crocodiles and mangrove flies, and with the fearful stench of the slime round you. What little time you have over you will employ in wondering why you came to West Africa, and why, after having reached this point of absurdity, you need have gone and painted the lily and adorned the rose, by being such a colossal ass as to come fooling about in mangrove swamps. On one occasion, a mighty Silurian, as *The Daily Telegraph* would call him, chose to get his front paws over the stern of my canoe, and endeavoured to improve our acquaintance. I had to retire to the bows, to keep the balance right,[1] and fetch him a clip on the snout with a paddle, when he withdrew, and I paddled into the very middle of the lagoon, hoping the water there was too deep for him or any of his friends to repeat the performance. Presumably it was, for no one did it again. I should think that crocodile was eight feet long; but don't go and say I measured him, or that this is my outside measurement for crocodiles. I have measured them when they have been killed by other people, fifteen, eighteen and twenty-one feet odd. This was only a pushing young creature who had not learnt manners.

Still, even if your own peculiar tastes and avocations do not take you in small dug-out canoes into the heart of the swamps, you can observe the difference in the local scenery made by the flowing of the tide when you

[1] It is no use saying because I was frightened, for this miserably understates the case.

are on a vessel stuck on a sand-bank, in the Rio del Rey for example. Moreover, as you will have little else to attend to, save mosquitoes and mangrove flies, when in such a situation, you may as well pursue the study. At the ebb gradually the foliage of the lower branches of the mangroves grows wet and muddy, until there is a great black band about three feet deep above the surface of the water in all directions; gradually a net-work of gray-white roots rises up, and below this again, gradually, a slope of smooth and lead-brown slime. The effect is not in the least as if the water had fallen, but as if the mangroves had, with one accord, risen up out of it, and into it again they seem silently to sink when the flood comes. But by this more safe, if still unpleasant, method of observing mangrove-swamps, you miss seeing in full the make of them, for away in their fastnesses the mangroves raise their branches far above the reach of tide line, and the great gray roots of the older trees are always sticking up in mid-air. But, fringing the rivers, there is always a hedge of younger mangroves whose lower branches get immersed.

At corners here and there from the river face you can see the land being made from the waters. A mud-bank forms off it, a mangrove seed lights on it, and the thing's done. Well! not done, perhaps, but begun; for if the bank is high enough to get exposed at low water, this pioneer mangrove grows. He has a wretched exist-ence though. You have only got to look at his dwarfed attenuated form to see this. He gets joined by a few more bold spirits and they struggle on together, their network of roots stopping an abundance of mud, and by good chance now and then a consignment of miscellaneous débris of palm leaves, or a floating tree-trunk, but they always die before they attain any considerable height. Still even in death they collect. Their bare white sticks remaining like a net gripped in the mud, so that these pioneer mangrove heroes may be said to have laid down their lives to make that mud-bank fit for colonisation, for the time gradually comes when other mangroves can and do colonise on it, and flourish, extending their territory steadily; and the mud-bank joins up with, and becomes a part of, Africa.

Right away on the inland fringe of the swamp – you may go some hundreds of miles before you get there – you can see the rest of the process. The mangroves there have risen up, and dried the mud to an extent that is more than good for themselves, have over civilised that mud in fact, and so the brackish waters of the tide – which, although their enemy when too deep or too strong in salt, is essential to their existence – cannot get to their roots. They have done this gradually, as a mangrove does all things, but they have done it, and down on to that mud come a whole set of palms from the old mainland, who in their early colonisation days go through similarly trying experiences. First the screw-pines come and live among them; then the wine-palm and various creepers, and then the oil-palm; and the débris of these plants being greater and making better soil than dead mangroves, they work quicker and the mangrove is doomed. Soon the salt waters are shut right out, the mangrove dies, and that bit of Africa is made. It is very interesting to get into these regions;

you see along the river-bank a rich, thick, lovely wall of soft-wooded plants, and behind this you find great stretches of death; – miles and miles sometimes of gaunt white mangrove skeletons standing on gray stuff that is not yet earth and is no longer slime, and through the crust of which you can sink into rotting putrefaction. Yet, long after you are dead, buried, and forgotten, this will become a forest of soft-wooded plants and palms; and finally of hard-wooded trees. Districts of this description you will find in great sweeps of Kama country for example, and in the rich low regions up to the base of the Sierra del Cristal and the Rumby range.

You often hear the utter lifelessness of mangrove-swamps commented on; why I do not know, for they are fairly heavily stocked with fauna, though the species are comparatively few. There are the crocodiles, more of them than any one wants; there are quantities of flies, particularly the big silent mangrove-fly which lays an egg in you under the skin; the egg becomes a maggot and stays there until it feels fit to enter into external life. Then there are 'slimy things that crawl with legs upon a slimy sea,' and any quantity of hopping mud-fish, and crabs, and a certain mollusc, and in the water various kinds of cat-fish. Birdless they are save for the flocks of gray parrots that pass over them at evening, hoarsely squarking; and save for this squarking of the parrots the swamps are silent all the day, at least during the dry season; in the wet season there is no silence night or day in West Africa, but that roar of the descending deluge of rain that is more monotonous and more gloomy than any silence can be. In the morning you do not hear the long, low, mellow whistle of the plantain-eaters calling up the dawn, nor in the evening the clock-bird nor the Handel-Festival-sized choruses of frogs, or the crickets, that carry on their vesper controversy of 'she did' – 'she didn't' so fiercely on hard land.

But the mangrove-swamp follows the general rule for West Africa, and night in it is noisier than the day. After dark it is full of noises; grunts from I know not what, splashes from jumping fish, the peculiar whirr of rushing crabs, and quaint creaking and groaning sounds from the trees; and – above all in eeriness – the strange whine and sighing cough of crocodiles. I shall never forget one moonlight night I spent in a mangrove-swamp. I was not lost, but we had gone away into the swamp from the main river, so that the natives of a village with an evil reputation should not come across us when they were out fishing. We got well in, on to a long pool or lagoon; and dozed off and woke, and saw the same scene around us twenty times in the night, which thereby grew into an æon, until I dreamily felt that I had somehow got into a world that was all like this, and always had been, and was always going to be so. Now and again the strong musky smell came that meant a crocodile close by, and one had to rouse up and see if all the crews' legs were on board, for Africans are reckless, and regardless of their legs during sleep. On one examination I found the leg of one of my most precious men ostentatiously sticking out over the side of the canoe. I woke him with a paddle, and said a few words regarding the inadvisability of wearing his leg like this in our situation; and he agreed with me, saying he had lost a valued uncle, who had been taken out of a canoe in this same swamp by a crocodile. His uncle's ghost had become, he said, a sort of devil which had been a trial to the family ever since; and he thought it must have pulled his leg out in the way I complained of, in order to get him to join him by means of another crocodile. I thanked him for the information and said it quite explained the affair, and I should do my best to prevent another member of the family from entering the state of devildom by aiming blows in the direction of any leg or arm I saw that uncle devil pulling out to place within reach of the crocodiles.

Great regions of mangrove-swamps are a characteristic feature of the West African Coast. The first of these lies north of Sierra Leone; then they occur, but of smaller dimensions – just fringes of river-outfalls – until you get to Lagos, when you strike the greatest of them all: – the swamps of the Niger outfalls (about twenty-three rivers in all) and of the Sombreiro, New Calabar, Bonny, San Antonio, Opobo (false and true), Kwoibo, Old Calabar (with the Cross Akwayafe Qwa Rivers) and Rio del Rey Rivers. The whole of this great stretch of coast is a mangrove-swamp, each river silently rolling down its great mass of mud-laden waters and constituting each in itself a very pretty problem to the navigator by its network of inter-communicating creeks, and the sand and mud bar which it forms off its entrance by dropping its heaviest mud; its lighter mud is carried out beyond its bar and makes the nasty-smelling brown soup of the South Atlantic Ocean, with froth floating in lines and patches on it, for miles to seaward.

In this great region of swamps every mile appears like every other mile until you get well used to it, and are able to distinguish the little local peculiarities at the entrance of the rivers and in the winding of the creeks, a thing difficult even for the most experienced navigator to do during those thick wool-like mists called smokes, which hang about the whole Bight from November till May (the dry season), sometimes lasting all day, sometimes clearing off three hours after sunrise.

The upper or north-westerly part of the swamp is round the mouths of the Niger, and it successfully concealed this fact from geographers down to 1830, when the series of heroic journeys made by Mungo Park, Clapperton, and the two Landers finally solved the problem – a problem that was as great and which cost more men's lives than even the discovery of the sources of the Nile.

That this should have been so may seem very strange to us who now have been told the answer to the riddle; for the upper waters of this great river were known of before Christ and spoken of by Herodotus, Pliny and Ptolemy, and its mouths navigated continuously along by the seaboard by trading vessels since the fifteenth century, but they were not recognised as belonging to the Niger. Some geographers held that the Senegal or the Gambia was its outfall; others that it was the Zaire (Congo); others that it did not come out on the West Coast at all, but got mixed up with the Nile in the middle of the continent, and so on. Yet when you come to know the swamps this is not so strange. You find on going up what looks like a big river – say Forcados, two and a half miles wide at the entrance and a real bit of the Niger. Before you are up it far great, broad, business-like-looking river entrances open on either side, showing wide rivers, mangrove-walled, but two-thirds of them are utter frauds which will ground you within half an hour of your entering them. Some few of them do communicate with other main channels to the great upper river, and others are main channels themselves; but most of them intercommunicate with each other and lead nowhere in particular, and you can't even get there because of their shallowness. It is small wonder that the earlier navigators did not get far up them in sailing ships, and that the problem had to be solved by men descending the main stream of the Niger before it commences to what we in Devonshire should call 'squander itself about' in all these channels. And in addition it must be remembered that the natives with whom these trading vessels dealt, first for slaves, afterwards for palm-oil, were not, and are not now, members of the Lo family of savages. Far from it: they do not go in for 'gentle smiles,' but for murdering any unprotected boat's crew they happen to come across, not only for a love of sport but to keep white traders from penetrating to the trade-producing interior, and spoiling prices. And the region is practically foodless. But I need not here go into further particulars regarding the discovery of the connection between the Niger and its delta. It is just the usual bad ju-ju of all big

African rivers. If you first find the mouth, as in the case of the Nile, you have awful times finding the source. If you find the upper waters, you have awful times in discovering the mouth. If you find a bit of its middle, like the Congo, you have awful times in both directions, but fortunately the Congo does play fair and does not go and split itself up and dive into a mass of mangrove-swamps like the Niger; so that bit of river work at least was easier.

The rivers of the great mangrove-swamp from the Sombreiro to the Rio del Rey are now known pretty surely not to be branches of the Niger, but the upper regions of this part of the Bight are much neglected by English explorers. I believe the great swamp region of the Bight of Biafra is the greatest in the world, and that in its immensity and gloom it has a grandeur equal to that of the Himalayas. I am not saying a beauty; I own I see a great beauty in it sometimes, but it is evidently not of a popular type, for I can never persuade my companions down in the Rivers to recognise it; still it produces an emotion in the stoutest-hearted among them; yea, even in those who have sailed the world round; who have cruised for years in the Southern seas, know their West Indies by heart, have run regularly for years to Rio de Janeiro, and have time and again been to where 'thy towers, they say, gleam fair, Bombay, across the deep blue sea.'

Take any such a man, educated or not, and place him on Bonny or Forcados River in the wet season on a Sunday – Bonny for choice. Forcados is good. You'll keep Forcados scenery 'indelibly limned on the tablets of your mind when a yesterday has faded from its page,' after you have spent even a week waiting for the Lagos branch-boat on its inky waters. But Bonny! Well, come inside the bar and anchor off the factories: seaward there is the foam of the bar gleaming and wicked – white against a leaden sky and what there is left of Breaker Island. In every other direction you will see the apparently endless walls of mangrove, unvarying in colour, unvarying in form, unvarying in height, save from perspective. Beneath and between you and them lie the rotting mud waters of Bonny River, and away up and down river, miles of rotting mud waters fringed with walls of rotting mud mangrove-swamp. The only break in them – one can hardly call it a relief to the scenery – are the gaunt black ribs of the old hulks, once used as trading stations, which lie exposed at low water near the shore, protruding like the skeletons of great unclean beasts who have died because Bonny water was too strong even for them.

Raised on piles from the mud shore you will see the white-painted factories and their great store-houses for oil; each factory likely enough with its flag at half-mast, which does not enliven the scenery either, for you know it is because somebody is 'dead again.' Throughout and over all is the torrential downpour of the wet-season rain, coming down night and day with its dull roar. I have known it rain six mortal weeks in Bonny River, just for all the world as if it were done by machinery, and the interval that came then was only a few wet days, whereafter it settled itself down to work again in the good West Coast waterspout pour for more weeks. I fancy junior clerks of the weather-department must be entrusted with the Bight of Biafra's weather, on account of its extreme simplicity; their duty is just to turn on so many months' wet, and then a tornado season – one tornado administered every forty-eight hours; then stop all water supply and turn on sun; then a tornado season as before, and back again to the water tap. But I cannot say I think the weather does them any credit. Tornados frequently come twice a day, and they frequently leave the water tap running a month more than they ought to. The senior clerks should attend to the matter, but presumably their time is taken up with complicated climates like England's.

While your eyes are drinking in the characteristics of Bonny scenery you notice a peculiar smell – an intensification of that smell you noticed when nearing Bonny, in the evening, out at sea. That's the breath of the malarial mud, laden with fever, and the chances are you will be down to-morrow. If it is near evening time now, you can watch it becoming incarnate, creeping and crawling and gliding out from the side creeks and between the mangrove-roots, laying itself upon the river, stretching and rolling in a kind of grim play, and finally crawling up the side of the ship to come on board and leave its cloak of moisture that grows green mildew in a few hours over all. Noise you will not be much troubled with: there is only that rain, a sound I have known make men who are sick with fever well-nigh mad, and now and again the depressing cry of the curlews which abound here. This combination is such that after six or eight hours of it you will be thankful to hear your shipmates start to work the winch.

[...]

Forest, Elephants and Gorillas

French Congo

I will not bore you with my diary in detail regarding our land journey, because the water-washed little volume attributive to this period is mainly full of reports of law cases, for reasons hereinafter to be stated; and at night, when passing through this bit of country, I was usually too tired to do anything more than make an entry such as: '5 S., 4 R. A., N. E. Ebony. T. 1–50, &c., &c.' – entries that require amplification to explain their significance, and I will proceed to explain.

Our first day's march was a very long one. Path in the ordinary acceptance of the term there was none. Hour after hour, mile after mile, we passed on, in the under-gloom of the great forest. The pace made by the Fans, who are infinitely the most rapid Africans I have ever come across, severely tired the Ajumba, who are canoe men, and who had been as fresh as paint, after their exceedingly long day's paddling from Arevooma to M'fetta. Ngouta, the Igalwa interpreter, felt pumped, and said as much, very early in the day. I regretted very much having brought him; for, from a mixture of nervous exhaustion arising from our M'fetta experiences, and a touch of chill, he had almost entirely lost his voice, and I feared would fall sick. The Fans were evidently quite at home in the forest, and strode on over fallen trees and rocks with an easy, graceful stride. What saved us weaklings was the Fans' appetites; every two hours they sat down, and had a snack of a pound or so of meat and aguma apiece, followed by a pipe of tobacco. We used to come up with them at these halts. Ngouta and the Ajumba used to sit down; and rest with them, and I also, for a few minutes, for a rest and chat, and then I would go on alone, thus getting a good start. I got a good start, in the other meaning of the word, on the afternoon of the first day when descending into a ravine.

I saw in the bottom, wading and rolling in the mud, a herd of five elephants. I am certain that owing to some misapprehension among the Fates I was given a series of magnificent sporting chances, intended as a special treat for some favourite Nimrod of those three ladies, and I know exactly how I ought to have behaved. I should have felt my favourite rifle fly to my shoulder, and then, carefully sighting for the finest specimen, have fired. The noble beast should have stumbled forward, recovered itself, and shedding its life blood behind it have crashed away into the forest. I should then have tracked it, and either with one well-directed shot have given it its quietus, or have got charged by it, the elephant passing completely over my prostrate body; either termination is good form, but I never have these things happen, and never will. (In the present case I remembered, hastily, that your one chance when charged by several elephants is to dodge them round trees, working down wind all the time, until they lose smell and sight of you, then to lie quiet for a time, and go home.) It was evident from the utter unconcern of these monsters that I was down wind now, so I had only to attend to dodging, and I promptly dodged round a tree, thinking perhaps a dodge in time saves nine – and I lay down. Seeing they still displayed no emotion on my account, and fascinated by the novelty of the scene, I crept forward from one tree to another, until I was close enough to have hit the nearest one with a stone, and spats of mud, which they sent flying with their stamping and wallowing came flap, flap among the bushes covering me.

One big fellow had a nice pair of 40 lb. or so tusks on him, singularly straight, and another had one big curved tusk and one broken one. If I were an elephant I think I would wear the tusks straight; they must be more effective weapons thus but there seems no fixed fashion among elephants here in this matter. Some of them lay right down like pigs in the deeper part of the swamp, some drew up trunkfuls of water and syringed themselves and each other, and every one of them indulged in a good rub against a tree. Presently when they had had enough of it they all strolled off up wind, a way elephants have; but why I do not know, because they know the difference, always carrying their trunk differently when they are going up wind to what they do when they are going down – arrested mental development, I suppose. They strolled through the bush in Indian file, now and then breaking off a branch, but leaving singularly little dead water for their tonnage and breadth of beam. One laid his trunk affectionately on the back of the one in front of him, which I believe to be the elephant equivalent to walking arm-in-arm. When they had gone I rose up, turned round to find the men, and trod on Kiva's back then and there, full and fair, and fell sideways down the steep hillside until I fetched up among some roots.

It seems Kiva had come on, after his meal, before the others, and seeing the elephants, and being a born hunter, had crawled like me down to look at them. He had not expected to find me there, he said. I do not believe he gave a thought of any sort to me in the presence of these fascinating creatures, and so he got himself trodden on. I suggested to him we should pile the baggage, and go and have an elephant hunt. He shook his head reluctantly, saying 'Kor, kor,' like a depressed rook, and explained we were not strong enough; there were only three Fans – the Ajumba, and Ngouta did not count – and moreover that we had not brought sufficient ammunition owing to the baggage having to be carried, and the ammunition that we had must be saved for other game than elephant, for we might meet war before we met the Rembwé River.

We had by now joined the rest of the party, and were all soon squattering about on our own account in the elephant bath. It was shocking bad going – like a ploughed field exaggerated by a terrific nightmare. It pretty nearly pulled all the legs off me, and to this hour I cannot tell you if it is best to put your foot into a footmark – a young pond, I mean – about the size of the bottom of a Madeira work arm-chair, or whether you should poise yourself on the rim of the same, and stride forward to its other bank boldly and hopefully. The footmarks and the places where the elephants had been rolling were by now filled with water, and the mud underneath was in places hard and slippery. In spite of my determination to preserve an awesome and unmoved calm while among these dangerous savages, I had to give way and laugh explosively; to see the portly, powerful Pagan suddenly convert himself into a quadruped, while Gray Shirt poised himself on one heel and waved his other leg in the air to advertise to the assembled nations that he was about to sit down, was irresistible. No one made such palaver about taking a seat as Gray Shirt; I did it repeatedly without any fuss to speak of. That lordly elephant-hunter, the Great Wiki, would, I fancy, have strode over safely and with dignity, but the man who was in front of him spun round on his own axis and flung his arms round the Fan, and they went to earth together; the heavy load on Wiki's back drove them into the mud like a pile-driver. However we got through in time, and after I had got up the other side of the ravine I saw the Fan let the Ajumba go on, and were busy searching themselves for something.

I followed the Ajumba, and before I joined them felt a fearful pricking irritation. Investigation of the affected part showed a tick of terrific size with its head embedded in the flesh; pursuing this interesting subject, I found three more, and had awfully hard work to get them off and painful too for they give one not only a feeling of irritation at their holding-on place, but a streak of rheumatic-feeling pain up from it. On completing operations I went on and came upon the Ajumba in a state more approved of by Praxiteles than by the general public nowadays. They had found out about elephant ticks so I went on and got an excellent start for the next stage.

By this time, shortly after noon on the first day, we had struck into a mountainous and rocky country, and also struck a track – a track you had to keep your eye on or you lost it in a minute, but still a guide as to direction.

The forest trees here were mainly ebony and great hard wood trees, with no palms save my old enemy the climbing palm, *calamus*, as usual, going on its long excursions, up one tree and down another, bursting into a plume of fronds, and in the middle of each plume one long spike sticking straight up, which was an unopened frond, whenever it got a gleam of sunshine; running along the ground over anything it meets, rock or fallen timber, all alike, its long, dark-coloured, rope-like stem simply furred with thorns. Immense must be the length of some of these climbing palms. One tree I noticed that day that had hanging from its summit, a good one hundred and fifty feet above us, a long straight rope-like palm stem. Interested, I went to it, and tried to track it to root, and found it was only a loop that came down from another tree. I had no time to trace it further; for they go up a tree and travel along the surrounding tree-tops, take an occasional dip, and then up again.

The character of the whole forest was very interesting. Sometimes for hours we passed among thousands upon thousands of gray-white columns of uniform height (about 100–150 feet); at the top of these the boughs branched out and interlaced among each other, forming a canopy or ceiling, which dimmed the light even of the equatorial sun to such an extent that no undergrowth could thrive in the gloom. The statement of the struggle for existence was published here in plain figures, but it was not, as in our climate, a struggle against climate mainly, but an internecine war from over population. Now and again we passed among vast stems of buttressed trees, sometimes enormous in girth; and from their far-away summits hung great bush-ropes, some as straight as plumb lines, others coiled round, and intertwined among each other, until one could fancy one was looking on some mighty battle between armies of gigantic serpents, that had been arrested at its height by some magic spell. All these bush-ropes were as bare of foliage as a ship's wire rigging, but a good many had thorns. I was very curious as to how they got up straight, and investigation showed me that many of them were carried up with a growing tree. The only true climbers were the *calamus* and the rubber vine (*Landolphia*), both of which employ hook tackle.

Some stretches of this forest were made up of thin, spindly stemmed trees of great height, and among these stretches I always noticed the ruins of some forest giant, whose death by lightning or by his superior height having given the demoniac tornado wind an extra grip on him, had allowed sunlight to penetrate the lower regions of the forest; and then evidently the seedlings and saplings, who had for years been living a half-starved life for light, shot up. They seemed to know that their one chance lay in getting with the greatest rapidity to the level of the top of the forest. No time to grow fat in the stem. No time to send out side branches, or any of those vanities. Up, up to the light level, and he among them who reached it first won in this game of life or death; for when he gets there he spreads out his crown of upper branches, and shuts off the life-giving sunshine from his competitors, who pale off and die, or remain dragging on an attenuated existence waiting for another chance, and waiting sometimes for centuries. There must be tens of thousands of seeds which perish before they get their chance; but the way the seeds of the hard wood African trees are packed, as it were, in cases specially made durable, is very wonderful. Indeed the ways of Providence here are wonderful in their strange dual intention to preserve and to destroy; but on the whole, as Peer Gynt truly observes, '*Ein guter Wirth – nein das ist er nicht.*'

We saw this influence of light on a large scale as soon as we reached the open hills and mountains of the Sierra del Cristal, and had to pass over those fearful avalanche-like timber falls on their steep sides. The worst of these lay between Efoua and Egaja, where we struck a part of the range that was exposed to the south-east. These falls had evidently arisen from the tornados, which from time to time have hurled down the gigantic trees whose hold on the superficial soil over the sheets of hard bed rock was insufficient, in spite of all the anchors they had out in the shape of roots and buttresses and all the rigging in the shape of bush ropes. Down they had come, crushing and dragging down with them those near them or bound to them by the great tough climbers.

Getting over these falls was perilous, not to say scratchy work. One or another member of our party always went through; and precious uncomfortable going it was I found, when I tried it in one above Egaja; ten or twelve feet of crashing creaking timber, and then flump on to a lot of rotten, wet débris, with more snakes and centipedes among it than you had any immediate use for, even though you were a collector; but there you had to stay, while Wiki, who was a most critical connoisseur, selected from the surrounding forest a bush-rope that he regarded as the correct remedy for the case, and then up you were hauled, through the sticks you had turned the wrong way on your down journey.

The Duke had a bad fall, going twenty feet or so before he found the rubbish heap; while Fika, who went through with a heavy load on his back, took us, on one occasion, half an hour to recover; and when we had just got him to the top, and able to cling on to the upper sticks, Wiki, who had been superintending operations, slipped backwards, and went through on his own account. The bush-rope we had been hauling on was too worn with the load to use again, and we just hauled Wiki out with the first one we could drag down and cut; and Wiki, when he came up, said we were reckless, and knew nothing of bush ropes, which shows how ungrateful an African can be. It makes the perspiration run down my nose whenever I think of it. The sun was out that day; we were neatly situated on the Equator, and the air was semi-solid, with the stinking exhalations from the swamps with which the mountain chain is fringed and intersected; and we were hot enough without these things, because of the violent exertion of getting these twelve to thirteen-stone gentlemen up among us again, and the fine varied exercise of getting over the fall on our own account.

When we got into the cool forest beyond it was delightful; particularly if it happened to be one of those lovely stretches of forest, gloomy down below, but giving hints that far away above us was a world of bloom and scent and beauty which we saw as much of as earth-worms in a flower-bed. Here and there the ground was strewn with great cast blossoms, thick, wax-like, glorious cups of orange and crimson and pure white, each one of which was in itself a handful, and which told us that some of the trees around us were showing a glory of colour to heaven alone. Sprinkled among them were bunches of pure stephanotis-like flowers, which said that the gaunt bush-ropes were rubber vines that had burst into flower when they had seen the sun. These flowers we came across in nearly every type of forest all the way, for rubber abounds here.

I will weary you no longer now with the different kinds of forest and only tell you I have let you off several. The natives have separate names for seven different kinds, and these might, I think, be easily run up to nine.

A certain sort of friendship soon arose between the Fans and me. We each recognised that we belonged to that same section of the human race with whom it is better to drink than to fight. We knew we would each have killed the other, if sufficient inducement were offered, and so we took a certain amount of care that the inducement should not arise. Gray Shirt and Pagan also, their trade friends, the Fans treated with an independent sort of courtesy; but Silence, Singlet, the Passenger, and above all Ngouta, they openly did not care a row of pins for, and I have small doubt that had it not been for us other three they would have killed and eaten these very amiable gentlemen with as much compunction as an English sportsman would kill as many rabbits. They on their part hated the Fan, and never lost an opportunity of telling me 'these Fan be bad man too much.' I must not forget to mention the other member of our party, a Fan gentleman with the manners of a duke and the habits of a dustbin. He came with us, quite uninvited by me, and never asked for any pay; I think he only wanted to see the fun, and drop in for a fight if there was one going on, and to pick up the pieces generally. He was evidently a man of some importance, from the way the others treated him; and moreover he had a splendid gun, with a gorilla skin sheath for its lock, and ornamented all over its stock with brass nails. His costume consisted of a small piece of dirty rag round his loins; and whenever we were going through dense undergrowth, or wading a swamp, he wore that filament tucked up scandalously short. Whenever we were sitting down in the forest having one of our nondescript meals, he always sat next to me and appropriated the tin. Then he would fill his pipe, and turning to me with the easy grace of aristocracy, would say what may be translated as 'My dear Princess, could you favour me with a lucifer?'

I used to say, 'My dear Duke, charmed, I'm sure,' and give him one ready lit.

I dared not trust him with the box whole, having a personal conviction that he would have kept it. I asked him what he would do suppose I was not there with a box of lucifers; and he produced a bush-cow's horn with a neat wood lid tied on with tie tie, and from out of it he produced a flint and steel and demonstrated. Unfortunately all his grace's minor possessions, owing to the scantiness of his attire, were in one and the same pine-apple-fibre bag which he wore slung across his shoulder; and these possessions, though not great, were as dangerous to the body as a million sterling is said to be to the soul, for they consisted largely of gunpowder and snuff, and their separate receptacles leaked and their contents commingled, so that demonstration on fire-making methods among the Fan ended in an awful bang and blow-up in a small way, and the Professor and his pupil sneezed like fury for ten minutes, and a cruel world laughed till it nearly died, for twenty. Still that bag with all its failings was a wonder for its containing power.

The first day in the forest we came across a snake – a beauty with a new red-brown and yellow-patterned velvety skin, about three feet six inches long and as thick as a man's thigh. Ngouta met it, hanging from a bough, and shot backwards like a lobster, Ngouta having among his many weaknesses a rooted horror of snakes. This snake the Ogowé natives all hold in great aversion. For the bite of other sorts of snakes they profess to have remedies, but for this they have none. If, however, a native is stung by one he usually conceals the fact that it was this particular kind, and tries to get any chance the native doctor's medicine may give. The Duke stepped forward and with one blow flattened its head against the tree with his gun butt, and then folded the snake up and got as much of it as possible into the bag, while the rest hung dangling out. Ngouta, not being able to keep ahead of the Duke, his Grace's pace being stiff, went to the extreme rear of the party, so that other people might be killed first if the snake returned to life, as he surmised it would. He fell into other dangers from this caution, but I cannot chronicle Ngouta's afflictions in full without running this book into an old-fashioned folio size. We had the snake for supper, that is to say the Fan and I; the others would not touch it, although a good snake, properly cooked, is one of the best meats one gets out here, far and away better than the African fowl.

The Fans also did their best to educate me in every way: they told me their names for things, while I told them mine, throwing in besides as 'a dash for top' a few colloquial phrases such as: 'Dear me, now,' 'Who'd have thought it,' 'Stuff, my dear sir,' and so on; and when I left them they had run each together as it were into one word, and a nice savage sound they had with them too, especially 'dearmenow,' so I must warn any philologist who visits the Fans, to beware of regarding any word beyond two syllables in length as being of native origin. I found several European words already slightly altered in use among them, such as 'Amuck' – a mug, 'Alas' – a glass, a tumbler. I do not know whether their 'Ami' – a person addressed, or spoken of – is French or not. It may come from 'Anwĕ' – M'pongwe for 'Ye,' 'You.' They use it as a rule in addressing a person after the phrase they always open up conversation with, 'Azuna' – Listen, or I am speaking.

They also showed me many things: how to light a fire from the pith of a certain tree, which was useful to me in after life, but they rather overdid this branch of instruction one way and another; for example, Wiki had, as above indicated, a mania for bush-ropes and a marvellous eye and knowledge of them; he would pick out from among the thousands surrounding us now one of such peculiar suppleness that you could wind it round anything, like a strip of cloth, and as strong withal as a hawser; or again another which has a certain stiffness, combined with a slight elastic spring, excellent for hauling, with the ease and accuracy of a lady who picks out the particular twisted strand of embroidery silk from a multi-coloured tangled ball. He would go into the bush after them while other people were resting, and particularly after the sort which, when split is bright yellow, and very supple and excellent to tie round loads.

On one occasion, between Egaja and Esoon, he came back from one of these quests and wanted me to come and see something, very quietly; I went, and we crept down into a rocky ravine, on the other side of which lay one of the outer-most Egaja plantations. When we got to the edge of the cleared ground, we lay down, and wormed our way, with elaborate caution, among a patch of Koko; Wiki first, I following in his trail.

After about fifty yards of this, Wiki sank flat, and I saw before me some thirty yards off, busily employed in pulling down plantains, and other depredations, five gorillas: one old male, one young male, and three females. One of these had clinging to her a young fellow, with beautiful wavy black hair with just a kink in it. The big male was crouching on his haunches, with his long arms hanging down on either side, with the backs of his hands on the ground, the palms upwards. The elder lady was tearing to pieces and eating a pine-apple, while the others were at the plantains destroying more than they ate.

They kept up a sort of a whinnying, chattering noise, quite different from the sound I have heard gorillas give when enraged, or from the one you can hear them giving when they are what the natives call 'dancing' at night. I noticed that their reach of arm was immense, and that when they went from one tree to another, they squattered across the open ground in a most in-elegant style, dragging their long arms with the knuckles downwards. I should think the big male and female were over six feet each. The others would be from four to five. I put out my hand and laid it on

Wiki's gun to prevent him from firing, and he, thinking I was going to fire, gripped my wrist.

I watched the gorillas with great interest for a few seconds, until I heard Wiki make a peculiar small sound, and looking at him saw his face was working in an awful way as he clutched his throat with his hand violently.

Heavens! think I, this gentleman's going to have a fit; it's lost we are entirely this time. He rolled his head to and fro, and then buried his face into a heap of dried rubbish at the foot of a plantain stem, clasped his hands over it, and gave an explosive sneeze. The gorillas let go all, raised themselves up for a second, gave a quaint sound between a bark and a howl, and then the ladies and the young gentleman started home. The old male rose to his full height (it struck me at the time this was a matter of ten feet at least, but for scientific purposes allowance must be made for a lady's emotions) and looked straight towards us, or rather towards where that sound came from. Wiki went off into a paroxysm of falsetto sneezes the like of which I have never heard; nor evidently had the gorilla, who doubtless thinking, as one of his black co-relatives would have thought, that the phenomenon favoured Duppy, went off after his family with a celerity that was amazing the moment he touched the forest, and disappeared as they had, swinging himself along through it from bough to bough, in a way that convinced me that, given the necessity of getting about in tropical forests, man has made a mistake in getting his arms shortened. I have seen many wild animals in their native wilds, but never have I seen anything to equal gorillas going through bush; it is a graceful, powerful, superbly perfect hand-trapeze performance.

[...]

3

Climbing the Great Peak of the Cameroons

i. The Throne of Thunder
German Kamerun

From the deck of the *Niger* I found myself again confronted with my great temptation – the magnificent Mungo Mah Lobeh – the Throne of Thunder. Now it is none of my business to go up mountains. There's next to no fish on them in West Africa, and precious little good rank fetish, as the population on them is sparse – the African, like myself, abhorring cool air. Nevertheless, I feel quite sure that no white man has ever looked on the great Peak of Cameroon without a desire arising in his mind to ascend it and know in detail the highest point on the western side of the continent, and indeed one of the highest points in all Africa. Do not, however, imagine that the ascent is a common incident in a coaster's life; far from it. The coaster as a rule resists the temptation of Mungo firmly, being stronger minded than I am; moreover, he is busy and only too often fever-stricken in the bargain. But I am the exception, I own, and I have given in to the temptation and am the third Englishman to ascend the

Peak and the first to have ascended it from the south-east face. The first man to reach the summit was Sir Richard Burton, accompanied by the great botanist, Gustav Mann. He went up, as did the succeeding twenty-five (mostly Germans) from Babundi; a place on the seashore to the west. The first expedition to reach the summit from the side I tackled it was composed of the first lieutenant and doctor of the German man-of-war *Hyæna*. These gentlemen had accomplished this feat a few weeks before I landed at Victoria to make my attempt. I go into these details so as to excuse myself for subsequently giving you a detailed account of the south-east face of Munga mah Lobeh.

So great is the majesty and charm of this mountain that the temptation of it is as great to me to-day as it was on the first day I saw it, when I was feeling my way down the West Coast of Africa on the S. S. *Lagos* in 1893, and it revealed itself by good chance from its surf-washed plinth to its sky-scraping summit. Certainly it is most striking when you see it first, as I first saw it, after coasting for weeks along the low shores and mangrove-fringed rivers of the Niger Delta. Suddenly, right up out of the sea, rises the great mountain to its 13,760 feet, while close at hand, to westward, towers the lovely island mass of Fernando Po to 10,190 feet. But every time you pass it by its beauty grows on you with greater and greater force, though it is never twice the same. Sometimes it is wreathed with indigo-black tornado clouds, sometimes crested with snow, sometimes softly gorgeous with gold, green, and rose-coloured vapours tinted by the setting sun, sometimes completely swathed in dense cloud so that you cannot see it at all; but when you once know it is there it is all the same, and you bow down and worship.

There are only two distinct peaks to this glorious thing that geologists brutally call the volcanic intrusive mass of the Cameroon Mountains, viz., Big Cameroon and Little Cameroon. The latter, Mungo Mah Etindeh, has not yet been scaled, although it is only 5,820 feet. One reason for this is doubtless that the few people in fever-stricken, over-worked West Africa who are able to go up mountains, naturally try for the adjacent Big Cameroon; the other reason is that Mungo Mah Etindeh, to which Burton refers as 'the awful form of Little Cameroon,' is mostly sheer cliff, and is from foot to summit clothed in an almost impenetrable forest. Behind these two mountains of volcanic origin, which cover an area on an isolated base of between 700 and 800 square miles in extent, there are distinctly visible from the coast two chains of mountains, or I should think one chain deflected, the so-called Rumby and Omon ranges. These are no relations of Mungo, being of very different structure and conformation; the geological specimens I have brought from them and from the Cameroons being identified by geologists as respectively schistose grit and vesicular lava.

After spending a few pleasant days in Cameroon River in the society of Frau Plehn, my poor friend Mrs Duggan having, I ought to say, departed for England on the death of her husband, I went round to Victoria, Ambas Bay, on the *Niger*, and in spite of being advised solemnly by Captain Davies to 'chuck it as it was not a picnic,' I started to attempt the Peak of Cameroons as follows.

September 20th, 1895. – Left Victoria at 7.30, weather fine. Herr von Lucke, though sadly convinced, by a series of experiments he has been carrying on ever since I landed, and I expect before, that you cannot be in three places at one time, is still trying to do so; or more properly speaking he starts an experiment series for four places, man-like; instead of getting ill as I should under the circumstances, and he kindly comes with me as far as the bridge across the lovely cascading Lukole River, and then goes back at about seven miles an hour to look after Victoria and his sick subordinates in detail.

I, with my crew, keep on up the grand new road the Government is making, which when finished is to go from Ambas Bay to Buea, 3,000 feet up on the mountain's side. This road is quite the most magnificent of roads, as regards breadth and general intention, that I have seen anywhere in West Africa, and it runs through a superbly beautiful country. It is, I should say, as broad as Oxford Street; on either side of it are deep drains to carry off the surface waters, with banks of varied beautiful tropical shrubs and ferns, behind which rise, 100 to 200 feet high, walls of grand forest, the column-like tree-stems either hung with flowering, climbing plants and ferns, or showing soft red and soft grey shafts sixty to seventy feet high without an interrupting branch. Behind this again rise the lovely foot hills of Mungo, high up against the sky, coloured the most perfect soft dark blue.

The whole scheme of colour is indescribably rich and full in tone. The very earth is a velvety red brown, and the butterflies – which abound – show themselves off in the sunlight, in their canary-coloured, crimson, and peacock-blue liveries, to perfection. After five minutes' experience of the road I envy those butterflies. I do not believe there is a more lovely road in this world, and besides, it's a noble and enterprising thing of a Government to go and make it, considering the climate and the country; but to get any genuine pleasure out of it, it is requisite to hover in a bird- or butterfly-like way, for of all the truly awful things to walk on, that road, when I was on it, was the worst.

Of course this arose from its not being finished, not having its top on in fact: the bit that was finished, and had got its top on, for half a mile beyond the bridge, you could go over in a Bath chair. The rest of it made you fit for one for the rest of your natural life, for it was one mass of broken lava rock, and here and there leviathan tree-stumps that had been partially blown up with gunpowder.

When we near the forest end of the road, it comes on to rain heavily, and I see a little house on the left-hand side, and a European engineer superintending a group of very cheerful natives felling timber. He most kindly invites me to take shelter, saying it cannot rain as heavily as this for long. My men also announce a desire for water, and so I sit down and chat with the engineer under the shelter of his verandah, while the men go to the water-hole, some twenty minutes off.

The engineer is an Alsatian, and has been engaged on the Congo Free State Railway, which he abandoned because they put him up at the end station, on those awful Palaballa mountains. Four men who were at the station died of fever and he got it himself, and applied for leave to go down to Matadi to see a doctor. His request was peremptorily refused, and he was told he must remain at his post until another engineer came up to take over charge. He stayed for some days waiting, but no one came or gave signs of coming, and he found the company had given all their employees orders that he was not to be allowed on a train, so he walked down to Matadi. How he did it, knowing that country, I cannot think, but he was exceedingly ill when he got there, as may easily be imagined, and as soon as he had sufficiently recovered, he came up to the Cameroons, and obtained his present appointment, after having been kept and nursed up in the hospital there, to his considerable surprise after his Congo experiences. He was not hopeful about the future of that Congo railroad, or of that of its directors. He quoted as one of the reasons for his leaving it the doubt that it would ever be finished. Indexplicable is man! Why he should have cared whether it was finished or not as long as it kept on paying him £1 a day, I do not know. He had kept a diary of the accidents, which averaged two a day, and usually took the form of something going off the line, because the railway engines used were so light as to be flighty, and not really powerful enough to take up more than two trucks at a time, though always expected to do so. The wages of the natives employed were from 1s. to 1s. 6d. a day; very high pay. The Chinamen imported as navvies were an awful nuisance, always making palaver. The Senegal men are dangerous, because the French officials on the line always support them against other white men, Senegalese being Frenchmen, just as Kruboys are Englishmen.

While I am getting this last news from the Congo, the rain keeps on pouring down. I presently see one of my men sitting right in the middle of the road on a rock, totally unsheltered, and a feeling of shame comes over me in the face of this black man's aquatic courage. Besides, Herr von Lucke had said I was sure to get half-drowned and catch an awful cold, so there is no use delaying. Into the rain I go, and off we start. I may remark I subsequently found that my aquatic underling was drunk. I conscientiously attempt to keep dry, by holding up an umbrella, knowing that though hopeless it is the proper thing to do.

We leave the road about fifty yards above the hut, turning into the unbroken forest on the right-hand side, and following a narrow, slippery, muddy, root-beset bush-path that was a comfort after the road. Presently we come to a lovely mountain torrent flying down over red-brown rocks in white foam; exquisitely lovely, and only a shade damper than the rest of things. Seeing this I solemnly fold up my umbrella and give it to Kefalla. My relations, nay, even Mrs Roy, who is blind to a large percentage of my imperfections, say the most scathing things about my behaviour with regard to water. But really my conduct is founded on sound principles. I know from a series of carefully conducted experiments, carried out on the Devonshire Lynn, that I cannot go across a river on slippery stepping-stones; therefore, knowing that attempts to keep my feet out of water only end in my placing the rest of my anatomy violently in, I take charge of Fate and wade.

This particular stream, too, requires careful wading, the rocks over which it flows being arranged in picturesque, but perilous confusion; however all goes well, and getting to the other side I decide to 'chuck it,' as Captain Davis would say, as to keeping dry, for the rain comes down heavier than ever.

Now we are evidently dealing with a foot-hillside, but the rain is too thick for one to see two yards in any direction, and we seem to be in a ghost-land forest, for the great palms and red-woods rise up in the mist before us, and fade out in the mist behind, as we pass on. The rocks which edge and strew the path at our feet are covered with exquisite ferns and mosses – all the most delicate shades of green imaginable, and here and there of absolute gold colour, looking as if some ray of sunshine had lingered too long playing on the earth, and had got shut off from heaven by the mist, and so lay nestling among the rocks until it might rejoin the sun.

The path now becomes an absolute torrent, with mud-thickened water, which cascades round one's ankles in a sportive way, and round one's knees in the hollows in the path. Five seconds after abandoning the umbrella I am wet through, but it is not uncomfortable at this temperature, something like that of a cucumber frame with the lights on, if you can clear your mind of all prejudice, as Dr Johnson says, and forget the risk of fever which saturation entails.

On we go, the path underneath the water seems a pretty equal mixture of rock and mud, but they are not evenly distributed. Plantations full of weeds show up on either side of us, and we are evidently now on the top of a foot-hill. I suspect a fine view of the sea could be obtained from here, if you have an atmosphere that is less than 99¾ per cent of water. As it is, a white sheet – or more properly speaking, considering its soft, stuffy woolliness, a white blanket – is stretched across the landscape to the south-west, where the sea would show.

We go down-hill now, the water rushing into the back of my shoes for a change. The path is fringed by high, sugar-cane-like grass which hangs across it in a lackadaisical way, swishing you in the face and cutting like a knife whenever you catch its edge, and pouring continually insidious rills of water down one's neck. It does not matter. The whole Atlantic could not get more water on to me than I have already got. Ever and again I stop and wring out some of it from my skirts, for it is weighty. One would not imagine that anything could come down in the way of water thicker than the rain, but it can. When one is on the top of the hills, a cold breeze comes through the mist chilling one to the bone, and bending the heads of the palm trees, sends down from them water by the bucketful with a slap; hitting or missing you as the case may be.

Both myself and my men are by now getting anxious

for our 'chop,' and they tell me, 'We look them big hut soon.' Soon we do look them big hut, but with faces of undisguised horror, for the big hut consists of a few charred roof-mats, &c., lying on the ground. There has been a fire in that simple savage home. Our path here is cut by one that goes east and west, and after a consultation between my men and the Bakwiri, we take the path going east, down a steep slope between weedy plantations, and shortly on the left shows a steep little hill-side with a long low hut on the top. We go up to it and I find it is the habitation of a Basel Mission black Bible-reader. He comes out and speaks English well, and I tell him I want a house for myself and my men, and he says we had better come and stay in this one. It is divided into two chambers, one in which the children who attend the mission-school stay, and wherein there is a fire, and one evidently the abode of the teacher. I thank the Bible-reader and say that I will pay him for the house, and I and the men go in streaming, and my teeth chatter with cold as the breeze chills my saturated garment while I give out the rations of beef, rum, blankets, and tobacco to the men. Then I clear my apartment out and attempt to get dry, operations which are interrupted by Kefalla coming for tobacco to buy firewood off the mission teacher to cook our food by.

Presently my excellent little cook brings in my food, and in with it come two mission teachers – our first acquaintance, the one with a white jacket, and another with a blue. They lounge about and spit in all directions, and then chiefs commence to arrive with their families complete, and they sidle into the apartment and ostentatiously ogle the demijohn of rum.

They are, as usual, a nuisance, sitting about on everything. No sooner have I taken an unclean-looking chief off the wood sofa, than I observe another one has silently seated himself in the middle of my open portmanteau. Removing him and shutting it up, I see another one has settled on the men's beef and rice sack.

It is now about three o'clock and I am still chilled to the bone in spite of tea. The weather is as bad as ever. The men say that the rest of the road to Buea is far worse than that which we have so far come along, and that we should never get there before dark, and 'for sure' should not get there afterwards, because by the time the dark came down we should be in 'bad place too much.' Therefore, to their great relief, I say I will stay at this place – Buana – for the night, and go on in the morning time up to Buea; and just for the present I think I will wrap myself up in a blanket and try and get the chill out of me, so I give the chiefs a glass of rum each, plenty of head tobacco, and my best thanks for their kind call, and then turn them and the expectorating mission teachers out. I have not been lying down five minutes on the plank that serves for a sofa by day and a bed by night, when Charles comes knocking at the door. He wants tobacco. 'Missionary man no fit to let we have firewood unless we buy em.' Give Charles a head and shut him out again, and drop off to sleep again for a quarter of an hour, then am aroused by some enterprising sightseers pushing open the window-shutters; when I look round there are a mass of black heads sticking through the window-hole. I tell them respectfully that the circus is closed for repairs, and fasten up the shutters, but sleep is impossible, so I turn out and go and see what those men of mine are after. They are comfortable enough round their fire, with their clothes suspended on strings in the smoke above them, and I envy them that fire. I then stroll round to see if there is anything to be seen, but the scenery is much like that you would enjoy if you were inside a blancmange. So as it is now growing dark I return to my room and light candles, and read Dr Günther on Fishes. If this sort of weather goes on I expect I shall specialise in fins and gills myself. Room becomes full of blacks. Unless you watch the door, you do not see how it is done. You look at a corner one minute and it is empty, and the next time you look that way it is full of rows of white teeth and watching eyes. The two mission teachers come in and make a show of teaching a child to read the Bible. I, having decided that it does not matter much what kind of fins you wear as they all work well, write up my log. About seven I get cook to make me some more tea, and shortly after find myself confronted with difficulties as to the disposal of the two mission teachers for the night. This class of man has no resource in him, and I think worse of the effects of mission-teaching than usual as I prepare to try and get a sleep; not an elaborate affair, I assure you, for I only want to wrap myself round in a blanket and lie on that plank, but the rain has got into the blankets and horror! there is no pillow. The mission men have cleared their bed paraphernalia right out.

Now you can do without a good many things, but not without a pillow, so hunt round to find something to make one with; find the Bible in English, the Bible in German, and two hymn-books, and a candle-stick. These seem all the small articles in the room – no, there is a parcel behind the books – mission teachers' Sunday trousers – make delightful arrangement of books bound round with trousers and the whole affair wrapped in one of my towels. Never saw till now advantage of Africans having trousers. Civilisation has its points after all. But it is no use trying to get any sleep until those men are quieter. The partition which separates my apartment from theirs is a bamboo and mat affair, straight at the top so leaving under the roof a triangular space above common to both rooms. Also common to both rooms are the smoke of the fire and the conversation. Kefalla is holding forth in a dogmatic way, and some of the others are snoring. There is a new idea in decoration along the separating wall. Mr Morris might have made something out of it for a dado. It is composed of an arrangement in line of stretched out singlets. Vaseline the revolver. Wish those men would leave off chattering. Kefalla seems to know the worst about most of the people, black and white, down in Ambas Bay, but I do not believe those last two stories. Evidently great jokes in next room now; Kefalla has thrown himself, still talking, in the dark, on to the top of one of the mission teachers. The women of the village outside have been keeping up, this hour and more, a most melancholy coo-ōoing. Those foolish creatures are evidently worrying about their husbands who have gone down to market in Ambas Bay, and who, they think, are lost in the bush. I have not a shadow of a doubt that those husbands who are not home by now are safely drunk in town, or reposing on the grand new road the kindly Government have provided for them, either in one of the side drains, or tucked in among the lava rock.

September 21st. – Coo-ōoing went on all-night. I was aroused about 9.30 P.M., by uproar in adjacent hut: one husband had returned in a bellicose condition and whacked his wives, and their squarks and squalls, instead of acting as a warning to the other ladies, stimulate the silly things to go on coo-ōoing louder and more entreatingly than ever, so that their husbands might come home and whack them too, I suppose, and whenever the unmitigated hardness of my plank rouses me I hear them still coo-ōoing.

No watchman is required to wake you in the morning on the top of a Cameroon foot-hill by 5.30, because about 4 A.M. the dank chill that comes before the dawn does so most effectively. One old chief turned up early out of the mist and dashed me a bottle of palm wine; he says he wants to dash me a fowl, but I decline, and accept two eggs, and give him four heads of tobacco.

The whole place is swathed in thick white mist through which my audience arrive. But I am firm with them, and shut up the doors and windows and disregard their bangings on them while I am dressing, or rather redressing. The mission teachers get in with my tea, and sit and smoke and spit while I have my breakfast. Give me cannibal Fans! I do not believe Blue

Jacket is a teacher at all, but a horrible Frankenstein parasite thing on White Jacket. He takes everything away from White Jacket as soon as I give it him: White Jacket feebly remonstrating. I see as we leave that he is taking the money I gave the latter *vi et armis* out of his pocket.

It is pouring with rain again now, and we go down the steep hillock to the path we came along yesterday, keep it until we come to where the old path cuts it, and then turn up to the right following the old path's course and leave Buana without a pang of regret. Our road goes N.E. Oh, the mud of it! Not the clearish cascades of yesterday but sticky, slippery mud, intensely sticky, and intensely slippery. The narrow path which is filled by this, is V-shaped underneath from wear, and I soon find the safest way is right through the deepest mud in the middle.

The white mist shuts off all details beyond ten yards in any direction. All we can see, as we first turn up the path, is a patch of kokos of tremendous size on our right. After this comes weedy plantation, and stretches of sword grass hanging across the road. The country is not so level as – or rather, I should say, more acutely unlevel than – that we came over yesterday. On we go, patiently doing our mud pulling through the valleys; toiling up a hillside among lumps of rock and stretches of forest, for we are now beyond Buana's plantations; and skirting the summit of the hill only to descend into another valley. Evidently this is a succession of foot-hills of the great mountain and we are not on its true face yet. As we go on they become more and more abrupt in form, the valleys mere narrow ravines. Evidently in the wet season (this is only the tornado season) each of these valleys is occupied by a raging torrent from the look of the confused water-worn boulders. Now among the rocks there are only isolated pools, for the weather for a fortnight before I left Victoria had been fairly dry, and this rich porous soil soaks up an immense amount of water. It strikes me as strange that when we are either going up or down the hills, the ground is less muddy than when we are skirting their summits, but as my brother would say, 'it is perfectly simple, if you think about it,' because on the inclines the rush of water clears the soil away down to the bed rock. There is an outcrop of clay down by Buana, but though that was slippery, it is nothing to the slipperiness of this fine, soft, red-brown earth that is the soil higher up, and also round Ambas Bay. This gets churned up into a sort of batter where there is enough water lying on it, and, when there is not, an ice slide is an infant to it.

My men and I flounder about; thrice one of them, load and all, goes down with a squidge and a crash into the side grass, and says 'damn!' with quite the European accent; as a rule, however, we go on in single file, my shoes giving out a mellifluous squidge, and their naked feet a squish, squash. The men take it very good temperedly, and sing in between accidents; I do not feel much like singing myself, particularly at one awful spot, which was the exception to the rule that ground at acute angles forms the best going. This exception was a long slippery slide down into a ravine with a long, perfectly glassy slope up out of it. I remember one of my tutors saying, 'Always when on a long march assume the attitude you feel most inclined to, as it is less tiring.' There could not be the least shadow of a doubt about your inclinations as to attitude here, nor to giving way to them, so we arrive at the bottom of that ravine in a fine confused heap. As for going up out of it, it was not mere inclination – it was passion that possessed you. What you wanted to do was to plant your nose against the hill-side and wave your normally earthward extremities in the air, particularly when you were near the middle of the slope, or close to the top. Two of the boys gave way to this impulse; I, of course, did not, but when I felt it coming on like a sort of fit, flung myself sideways into the dense bush that edges the path, and when it had passed off, scrambled out and had another try at the slide.

After this we have a stretch of rocky forest, and pass by a widening in the path which I am told is a place where men blow, i.e., rest, and then pass through another a little further on, which is Buea's bush market. Then through an opening in the great war-hedge of Buea, a growing stockade some fifteen feet high, the lower part of it wattled. Close by is a cross put up to mark the spot where that gallant young German officer fell last January twelvemonth, when on the first expedition to open up this side of the mountain.

At the sides of the path here grow banks of bergamot and balsam, returning good for evil and smiling sweetly as we crush them. Thank goodness we are in forest now, and we seem to have done with the sword-grass.

The rocks are covered with moss and ferns, and the mist curling and wandering about among the stems is very lovely. I have to pause in life's pleasures because I want to measure one of the large earthworms, which, with smaller sealing-wax-red worms, are crawling about the path. He was eleven inches and three-quarters. He detained me some time getting this information, because he was so nervous during the operation.

In our next ravine there is a succession of pools, part of a mountain torrent of greater magnitude evidently than those we have passed, and in these pools there are things swimming. Spend more time catching them, with the assistance of Bum. I do not value Kefalla's advice, ample though it is, as being of any real value in the affair. Bag some water-spiders and two small fish. The heat is less oppressive than yesterday. All yesterday one was being alternately smothered in the valley and chilled on the hill-tops. To-day it is a more level temperature, about 70°, I fancy.

The soil up here, about 2,500 feet above sea-level, though rock-laden is exceedingly rich, and the higher we go there is more bergamot, native indigo, with its under-leaf dark blue, and lovely coleuses with red markings on their upper leaves, and crimson linings. I, as an ichthyologist, am in the wrong paradise. What a region this would be for a botanist!

The country is gloriously lovely if one could only see it for the rain and mist; but one only gets dim hints of its beauty when some cold draughts of wind come down from the great mountains and seem to push open the mist-veil as with spirit hands, and then in a minute let it fall together again. I do not expect to reach Buea within regulation time, but at 11.30 my men say 'we close in,' and then, coming along a forested hill and down a ravine, we find ourselves facing a rushing river, wherein a squad of black soldiers are washing clothes, with the assistance of a squad of black ladies, with much uproar and sky-larking. I hesitate on the bank. I am in an awful mess – mud-caked skirts, and blood-stained hands and face. Shall I make an exhibition of myself and wash here, or make an exhibition of myself by going unwashed to that unknown German officer who is in charge of the station? Naturally I wash here, standing in the river and swishing the mud out of my skirts; and then wading across to the other bank, I wring out my skirts, but what is life without a towel? The ground on the further side of the river is cleared of bush, and only bears a heavy crop of balsam; a few steps onwards bring me in view of a corrugated iron-roofed, plank-sided house, in front of which, towards the great mountain which now towers up into the mist, is a low clearing with a quadrangle of native huts – the barracks.

I receive a most kindly welcome from a fair, grey-eyed German gentleman, only unfortunately I see my efforts to appear before him clean and tidy have been quite unavailing, for he views my appearance with unmixed horror, and suggests an instant hot bath. I decline. Men can be trying! How in the world is any one going to take a bath in a house with no doors, and only very sketchy wooden window-shutters?

The German officer is building the house quickly,

as Ollendorff would say, but he has not yet got to such luxuries as doors, and so uses army blankets strung across the doorway; and he has got up temporary wooden shutters to keep the worst of the rain out, and across his own room's window he has a frame covered with greased paper. Thank goodness he has made a table, and a bench, and a washhand-stand out of planks for his spare room, which he kindly places at my disposal; and the Fatherland has evidently stood him an iron bedstead and a mattress for it. But the Fatherland is not spoiling or cosseting this man to an extent that will enervate him in the least.

I get the loads brought into my room, where they steam and distil rills of water on to the bare floor, and then, barricading the door-blankets and the window-shutters, I dispossess myself of the German territory I have acquired during the last twenty-four hours, and my portmanteau having kept fairly watertight, I appear as a reasonable being before society – i.e., Herr Liebert, the German officer – and hunt up my boys to get me tea. This being done, I go out on the verandah and discourse.

Society has got a dreadfully bad foot; weeks ago he injured it on the road, and then in cleaning out a bad sore on one of the men some of the purulent matter got into the wound, and consequently he has nearly lost his leg, or more properly speaking his life, for he lay thirteen days in bed, and there was no doctor even down in Victoria to take the leg off, if it had turned to gangrene, as it seemed likely to do. He makes nothing of it, and hops about in a most energetic way, looking after seventy black soldiers and their wives and children, giving them out their rations, drilling them, doctoring them, and everything else, and hankering to do more. Many of the soldiers are down with bad feet, in consequence of the badness of the roads hereabouts. These soldiers are an assortment of Wei-Weis and Su-Su from Sierra Leone, and some Yorubas. They are smart men and well cared for, and their uniforms far more reasonable and military than the absurd uniforms we put our Haussas into in Calabar, only the Fatherland ordains that they shall wear braces, and these unnecessary articles for an African are worn flowing free, except by those men actually on duty.

The mist clears off in the evening about five, and the surrounding scenery is at last visible. Fronting the house there is the cleared quadrangle, facing which on the other three sides are the lines of very dilapidated huts, and behind these the ground rises steeply, the great S.E. face of Mungo Mah Lobeh. It looks awfully steep when you know you have got to go up it. This station at Buea is 3,000 feet above sea-level, which explains the hills we have had to come up. The mountain wall when viewed from Buea is very grand, although it lacks snow-cap or glacier, and the highest summits of Mungo are not visible because we are too close under them, but its enormous bulk and its isolation make it highly impressive. The forest runs up it in a great band above Buea, then sends up great tongues into the grass belt above. But what may be above this grass belt I know not yet, for our view ends at the top of the wall of the great S.E. crater. My men say there are devils and gold up beyond, but the German authorities do not support this view. Those Germans are so sceptical. This station is evidently on a ledge, for behind it the ground falls steeply, and you get an uninterrupted panoramic view of the Cameroon estuary and the great stretches of low swamp lands with the Mungo and the Bimbia rivers, and their many creeks and channels, and far away east the strange abrupt forms of the Rumby Mountains. Herr Liebert says you can see Cameroon Government buildings from here, if only the day is clear, though they are some forty miles away. This view of them is, save a missionary of the Basel mission, the only white society available at Buea. Society here says the intercourse, though better than none, is slow. I suggest he should pay calls and indulge in conversation by means of a code of fire-works. 'Ha!' says he, 'you're like the Calabar major.' 'Which one?' say I, for there are majors and majors. 'The one who came here last dry season,' he said, 'and who went up on to the wall and set the grass on fire to show how he was going on, and had to run down for his life.' I know that man, and a very excellent man he is, but he is not in Calabar, nor is he a major; but society everywhere makes mistakes in technical things.

I hear more details about the death of poor Freiherr von Gravenreuth, whose fine monument of a seated lion I saw in the Government House grounds in the Cameroons the other day. Bush fighting in these West African forests is dreadfully dangerous work. Hemmed in by bush, in a narrow path along which you must pass slowly in single file, you are a target for all and any natives invisibly hidden in the undergrowth; and the war-hedge of Buea must have made an additional danger and difficulty here for the attacking party. The lieutenant and his small band of black soldiers had, after a stiff fight, succeeded in forcing the entrance to this, when their ammunition gave out, and they had to fall back. The Bueans, regarding this as their victory, rallied, and a chance shot killed the lieutenant instantly. A further expedition was promptly sent up from Victoria and it wiped the error out of the Buean mind and several Bueans with it. But it was a very necessary expedition. These natives were a constant source of danger to the more peaceful trading tribes, whom they would not permit to traverse their territory. The Bueans have been dealt with mercifully by the Germans, for their big villages, like Sapa, are still standing, and a continual stream of natives come into the barrack-yard, selling produce, or carrying it on down to Victoria markets, in a perfectly content and cheerful way. I met this morning a big burly chief with his insignia of office – a great stick. He, I am told, is the chief or Sapa whom Herr von Lucke has called to talk some palaver with down in Victoria.

At last I leave Herr Liebert, because everything I say to him causes him to hop, flying somewhere to show me something, and I am sure it is bad for his foot. I go and see that my men are safely quartered. Kefalla is laying down the law in a most didactic way to the soldiers. Herr Liebert has christened him 'the Professor,' and I adopt the name for him, but I fear 'Windbag' would fit him better.

At 7.30 a heavy tornado comes rolling down upon us. Masses of indigo cloud with livid lightning flashing in the van, roll out from over the wall of the great crater above; then with that malevolence peculiar to the tornado it sees all the soldiers and their wives and children sitting happily in the barrack yard, howling in a minor key and beating their beloved tom-toms, so it comes and sits flump down on them with deluges of water, and sends its lightning running over the ground in livid streams of living death. Oh they are nice things are tornadoes! I wonder what they will be like when we are up in their home; up atop of that precious wall? I had no idea Mungo was so steep. If I had – well, I am in for it now!

ii. The Ascent

September 22nd. – Wake at 5. Fine morning. Fine view towards Cameroon River. The broad stretch of forest below, and the water-eaten mangrove swamps below that, are all a glorious indigo flushed with rose colour from 'the death of the night,' as Kiva used to call the dawn. No one stirring till six, when people come out of the huts, and stretch themselves and proceed to begin the day, in the African's usual perfunctory, listless way. I am not stating this as a peculiar trait arising from his cerebral development; it is merely the natural sequence of the nights he goes in for so cheerily: *Katzenjammer*, is, I believe, the technical term.

My crew are worse than the rest. I go and hunt cook out. He props open one eye, with difficulty, and yawns a yawn that nearly cuts his head in two. I wake him up with a shock, by saying I mean to go on up to-day, and want my chop, and to start on time. He goes off and announces my horrible intention to the others. Kefalla soon arrives upon the scene full of argument, 'You no sabe this be Sunday, Ma?' says he in a tone that tells he considers this settles the matter. I 'sabe' unconcernedly; Kefalla scratches his head for other argument, but he has opened with his heavy artillery; which being repulsed throws his rear lines into confusion. Bum, the head man, then turns up, sound asleep inside, but quite ready to come. Bum, I find, is always ready to do what he is told, but has no more original ideas in his head than there are in a chair leg. Kefalla, however, by scratching other parts of his anatomy diligently, has now another argument ready, the two Bakwiris are sick with abdominal trouble, that requires rum and rest, and one of the other boys has hot foot.

Herr Liebert now appears upon the scene, and says I can have some of his labourers, who are now more or less idle, because he cannot get about much with his bad foot to direct them, so I give the Bakwiris and the two hot foot cases 'books' to take down to Herr von Lucke who will pay them off for me, and seeing that they have each a good day's rations of rice, beef, &c., eliminate them from the party.

In addition to the labourers, I am to have as a guide Sasu, a black sergeant, who went up the Peak with the officers of the *Hyæna*, and I get my breakfast, and then hang about watching my men getting ready very slowly to start. They spin some plausible yarns about getting food cooked, in case they cannot get a fire when we reach the top of the forest belt, where we are to camp. I never saw a forest yet in Africa where you could not get a fire, but knowing that my previous experiences have never been beyond 5,000 feet in elevation, I let them have their way. Off we get about 8, and start with all good wishes, and grim prophecies, from Herr Liebert.

Led by Sasu, and accompanied by 'To-morrow,' a man who has come to Buea from some interior unknown district, and who speaks no known language, and whose business it is to help to cut a way through the bush, we go down the path we came and cross the river again. This river seems to separate the final mass of the mountain from the foot-hills on this side. Immediately after crossing it we turn up into the forest on the right hand side, and 'To-morrow' cuts through an overgrown track for about half-an-hour, and then leaves us.

Everything is reeking wet, and we swish through thick undergrowth and then enter a darker forest where the earth is rocky and richly decorated with ferns and moss. For the first time in my life I see tree-ferns growing wild in luxuriant profusion. What glorious creations they are! Then we get out into the middle of a koko plantation. Next to sweet-potatoes, the premier abomination to walk through, give me kokos for good all-round tryingness, particularly when they are wet, as is very much the case now. These gigantic arums poise in their broad leaves little reservoirs of water, which you upset over yourself as you pass through. The big round roots are excellent things to fall over. They project above the earth, and you can jam your foot against them and pitch forward, or you can step on one of them and fall backwards or sideways. The entertainment they afford the wayfarer is not monotonous, but it is exasperating. Getting through these we meet the war hedge again, and after a conscientious struggle with various forms of vegetation in a muddled, tangled state, Sasu says, 'No good, path done got stopped up,' so we turn and retrace our steps all the way, cross the river, and horrify Herr Liebert by invading his house again. We explain the situation. Grave headshaking between him and Sasu about the practicability of any other route, because there is no other path. I do not like to say 'so much the better,' because it would have sounded ungrateful, but I knew from my Ogowé experiences that a forest that looks from afar a dense black mat is all right underneath, and there is a short path recently cut by Herr Liebert that goes straight up towards the forest above us. It had been made to go to a clearing, where ambitious agricultural operations were being inaugurated, when Herr Liebert hurt his foot. Up this we go, it is semi-vertical while it lasts, and it ends in a scrubby patch that is to be a plantation; this crossed we are in the *Urwald*, and it is more exquisite than words can describe, but not good going, particularly at one spot where a gigantic tree has fallen down across a little rocky ravine, and has to be crawled under. It occurs to me that this is a highly likely place for snakes, and an absolutely sure find for scorpions, and when we have passed it three of these latter interesting creatures are observed on the load of blankets which is fastened on to the back of Kefalla. We inform Kefalla of the fact on the spot. A volcanic eruption of entreaty, advice, and admonition results, but we still hesitate. However, the gallant cook tackles them in a sort of tip-cat way with a stick, and we proceed into a patch of long grass, beyond which there is a reach of amomums. The winged amomum I see here in Africa for the first time. Horrid slippery things amomum sticks to walk on, when they are lying on the ground; and there is a lot of my old enemy the calamus about.

On each side are deep forested dells and ravines, and rocks show up through the ground in every direction, and things in general are slippery, and I wonder now and again, as I assume with unnecessary violence a recumbent position, why I came to Africa; but patches of satin-leaved begonias and clumps of lovely tree-ferns reconcile me to my lot. Cook does not feel these forest charms, and gives me notice after an hour's experience of mountain forest-belt work; what cook would not?

As we get higher we have to edge and squeeze every few minutes through the aërial roots of some tremendous kind of tree, plentiful hereabouts. One of them we passed through I am sure would have run any Indian banyan hard for extent of ground covered, if it were measured. In the region where these trees are frequent, the undergrowth is less dense than it is lower down.

Imagine a vast, seemingly limitless cathedral with its countless columns covered, nay, composed of the most exquisite dark-green, large-fronded moss, with here and there a delicate fern embedded in it as an extra decoration. The white, gauze-like mist comes down from the upper mountain towards us: creeping, twining round, and streaming through the moss-covered tree columns – long bands of it reaching along sinuous, but evenly, for fifty and sixty feet or more, and then ending in a puff like the smoke of a gun. Soon, however, all the mist-streams coalesce and make the atmosphere all their own, wrapping us round in a clammy, chill embrace; it is not that wool-blanket, smothering affair that we were wrapped in down by Buana, but exquisitely delicate. The difference it makes to the beauty of the forest is just the same difference you would get if you put a delicate veil over a pretty woman's face or a sack over her head. In fact, the mist here was exceedingly becoming to the forest's beauty. Now and again growls of thunder roll out from, and quiver in the earth beneath our feet. Mungo is making a big tornado, and is stirring and simmering it softly so as to make it strong. I only hope he will not overdo it, as he does six times in seven, and make it too heavy to get out on to the Atlantic, where all tornadoes ought to go. If he does the thing will go and burst on us in this forest to-night.

The forest now grows less luxuriant though still close – we have left the begonias and the tree-ferns, and are in another zone. The trees now, instead of being clothed in rich, dark-green moss, are heavily festooned with long, greenish-white lichen. It pours with rain.

At last we reach the place where the sergeant says we ought to camp for the night. I have been feeling the time for camping was very ripe for the past hour, and Kefalla openly said as much an hour and a half ago, but he got such scathing things said to him about civilians' legs by the sergeant that I did not air my own opinion.

We are now right at the very edge of the timber belt. My head man and three boys are done to a turn. If I had had a bull behind me or Mr Fildes in front, I might have done another five or seven miles, but not more.

The rain comes down with extra virulence as soon as we set to work to start the fire and open the loads. I and Peter have great times getting out the military camp-bed from its tight, bolster-like case, while Kefalla gives advice, until, being irritated by the bed's behaviour, I blow up Kefalla and send him to chop fire-wood. However, we get the thing out and put up after cutting a place clear to set it on: owing to the world being on a stiff slant hereabouts, it takes time to make it stand straight. I get four stakes cut, and drive them in at the four corners of the bed, and then stretch over it Herr von Lucke's waterproof ground-sheet, guy the ends out to pegs with string, feel profoundly grateful to both Herr Liebert for the bed and Herr von Lucke for the sheet, and place the baggage under the protection of the German Government's two belongings. Then I find the boys have not got a fire with all their fuss, and I have to demonstrate to them the lessons I have learnt among the Fans regarding fire-making. We build a fire-house and then all goes well. I notice they do not make a fire Fan fashion, but build it in a circle.

Evidently one of the labourers from Buea, named Xenia, is a good man. Equally evidently some of my other men are only fit to carry sandwich-boards for Day and Martin's blacking. I dine luxuriously off tinned fat pork and hot tea, and then feeling still hungry go on to tinned herring. Excellent thing tinned herring, but I have to hurry because I know I must go up through the edge of the forest on to the grass land, and see how the country is made during the brief period of clearness that almost always comes just before nightfall. So leaving my boys comfortably seated round the fire having their evening chop, I pass up through the heavily lichen-tasselled fringe of the forest-belt into deep jungle grass, and up a steep and slippery mound. In front the mountain-face rises like a wall from behind a set of hillocks, similar to the one I am at present on. The face of the wall to the right and left has two dark clefts in it. The peak itself is not visible from where I am; it rises behind and beyond the wall. I stay taking compass bearings and look for an easy way up for to-morrow. My men, by now, have missed their 'ma' and are yelling for her dismally, and the night comes down with great rapidity for we are in the shadow of the great mountain mass, so I go back into camp. Alas! how vain are often our most energetic efforts to remove our fellow creatures from temptation. I knew a Sunday down among the soldiers would be bad for my men, and so came up here, and now, if you please, these men have been at the rum, because Bum, the head man, has been too done up to do anything but lie in his blanket and feed. Kefalla is laying down the law with great detail and unction. Cook who has been very low in his mind all day, is now weirdly cheerful, and sings incoherently. The other boys, who want to go to sleep, threaten to 'burst him' if he 'no finish.' It's no good – cook carols on, and soon succumbing to the irresistible charm of music, the other men have to join in the choruses. The performance goes on for an hour, growing woollier and woollier in tone, and then dying out in sleep.

I write by the light of an insect-haunted lantern, sitting on the bed, which is tucked in among the trees some twenty yards away from the boys' fire. There is a bird whistling in a deep rich note that I have never heard before.

September 23rd. – Morning gloriously fine. Rout the

boys out, and start at seven, with Sasu, Head man, Xenia, Black boy, Kefalla and Cook.

The great south-east wall of the mountain in front of us is quite unflecked by cloud, and in the forest are thousands of bees. We notice that the tongues of forest go up the mountain in some places a hundred yards or more above the true line of the belt. These tongues of forest get more and, more heavily hung with lichen, and the trees thinner and more stunted, towards their ends. I think that these tongues are always in places where the wind does not get full play. All those near our camping place on this south-east face are so. It is evidently not a matter of soil, for there is ample soil on this side above where the trees are, and then again on the western side of the mountain – the side facing the sea – the timber line is far higher up than on this. Nor, again, is it a matter of angle that makes the timber line here so low, for those forests on the Sierra del Cristal were growing luxuriantly over far steeper grades. There is some peculiar local condition just here evidently, or the forest would be up to the bottom of the wall of the crater. I am not unreasonable enough to expect it to grow on that, but its conduct in staying where it does requires explanation.

We clamber up into the long jungle grass region and go on our way across a series of steep-sided, rounded grass hillocks, each of which is separated from the others by dry, rocky watercourses. The effects produced by the seed-ears of the long grass round us are very beautiful; they look a golden brown, and each ear and leaf is gemmed with dew-drops, and those of the grass on the sides of the hillocks at a little distance off show a soft brown-pink.

After half an hour's climb, when we are close at the base of the wall, I observe the men ahead halting, and coming up with them find Monrovia Boy down a hole; a little deep blow-hole, in which, I am informed, water is supposed to be. But Monrovia soon reports 'No live.'

I now find we have not a drop of water, either with us or in camp, and now this hole has proved dry. There is, says the sergeant, no chance of getting any more water on this side of the mountain, save down at the river at Buea.

This means failure unless tackled, and it is evidently a trick played on me by the boys, who intentionally failed to let me know of this want of water before leaving Buea, where it seems they have all learnt it. Had I known, of course I should have brought up a sufficient supply. Now they evidently think that there is nothing to be done but to return to Buea, and go down to Victoria, and get their pay, and live happily ever after, without having to face the horror of the upper regions of the mountain. They have worked their oracle with other white folk, I find, for they quote the other white folk's docile conduct as an example to me. I express my opinion of them and of their victims in four words – send Monrovia boy, who I know is to be trusted, back to Buea with a scribbled note to Herr Liebert asking him to send me up two demijohns of water. I send cook with him as far as the camp in the forest we have just left with orders to bring up three bottles of soda water I have left there, and to instruct the men there that as soon as the water arrives from Buea they are to bring it on up to the camp I mean to make at the top of the wall.

The men are sulky, and Sasu, Peter, Kefalla, and head man say they will wait and come on as soon as cook brings the soda water, and I go on, and presently see Xenia and Black boy are following me. We get on to the intervening hillocks and commence to ascend the face of the wall.

The angle of this wall is great, and its appearance from below is impressive from its enormous breadth, and its abrupt rise without bend or droop for a good 2,000 feet into the air. It is covered with short, yellowish grass through which the burnt-up, scoriaceous lava rock protrudes in rough masses.

I got on up the wall, which when you are on it is not so perpendicular as it looks from below, my desire being to see what sort of country there was on the top of it, between it and the final peak. Sasu had reported to Herr Liebert that it was a wilderness of rock, in which it would be impossible to fix a tent, and spoke vaguely of caves. Here and there on the way up I come to holes, similar to the one my men had been down for water. I suppose these holes have been caused by gases from an under hot layer of lava bursting up through the upper cool layer. As I get higher, the grass becomes shorter and more sparse, and the rocks more ostentatiously displayed. Here and there among them are sadly tried bushes, bearing a beautiful yellow flower, like a large yellow wild rose, only scentless. It is not a rose at all, I may remark. The ground, where there is any basin made by the rocks, grows a great sedum, with a grand head of whity-pink flower, also a tall herb, with soft downy leaves silver grey in colour, and having a very pleasant aromatic scent, and here and there patches of good honest parsley. Bright blue, flannelly-looking flowers stud the grass in sheltered places and a very pretty large green orchid is plentiful. Above us is a bright blue sky with white cloud rushing hurriedly across it to the N.E. and a fierce sun. When I am about half-way up, I think of those boys, and, wanting rest, sit down by an inviting-looking rock grotto, with a patch of the yellow flowered shrub growing on its top. Inside it grow little ferns and mosses, all damp; but alas! no water pool, and very badly I want water by this time.

Below me a belt of white cloud had now formed, so that I could see neither the foot-hillocks nor the forest, and presently out of this mist came Xenia toiling up, carrying my black bag. 'Where them Black boy live?' said I. 'Black boy say him foot be tire too much,' said Xenia, as he threw himself down in the little shade the rock could give. I took a cupful of sour claret out of the bottle in the bag, and told Xenia to come on up as soon as he was rested, and meanwhile to yell to the others down below and tell them to come on. Xenia did, but sadly observed, 'softly softly still hurts the snail,' and I left him and went on up the mountain.

When I had got to the top of the rock under which I had sheltered from the blazing sun, the mist opened a little, and I saw my men looking like as many little dolls. They were still sitting on the hillock where I had left them. Buea showed from this elevation well. The guard house and the mission house, like little houses in a picture, and the make of the ground on which Buea station stands, came out distinctly as a ledge or terrace, extending for miles N.N.E. and S.S.W. This ledge is a strange-looking piece of country, covered with low bush, out of which rise great, isolated, white-stemmed cotton trees. Below, and beyond this is a denser band of high forest, and again below this stretches the vast mangrove-swamp fringing the estuary of the Cameroons, Mungo, and Bimbia rivers. It is a very noble view, giving one an example of the peculiar beauty one oft-times gets in this West African scenery, namely colossal sweeps of colour. The mangrove-swamps looked to-day like a vast damson-coloured carpet threaded with silver where the waterways ran. It reminded me of a scene I saw once near Cabinda, when on climbing to the top of a hill I suddenly found myself looking down on a sheet of violet pink more than a mile long and half a mile wide. This was caused by a climbing plant having taken possession of a valley full of trees, whose tops it had reached and then spread and interlaced itself over them, to burst into profuse glorious laburnum-shaped bunches of flowers.

After taking some careful compass bearings for future use regarding the Rumby and Omon range of mountains, which were clearly visible and which look fascinatingly like my beloved Sierra del Cristal, I turned my face to the wall of Mungo, and continued the ascent. The sun, which was blazing, was reflected back from the rocks in scorching rays. But it was more bearable now, because its heat was tempered by a bitter wind.

The slope becoming steeper, I gradually made my way towards the left until I came to a great lane, as neatly walled with rock as if it had been made with human hands. It runs down the mountain face, nearly vertically in places and at stiff angles always, but it was easier going up this lane than on the outside rough rock, because the rocks in it had been smoothed by mountain torrents during thousands of wet seasons, and the walls protected one from the biting wind, a wind that went through me, for I had been stewing for nine months and more in tropic and equatorial swamps.

Up this lane I went to the very top of the mountain wall, and then, to my surprise, found myself facing a great, hillocky, rock-encumbered plain, across the other side of which rose the mass of the peak itself, not as a single cone, but as a wall surmounted by several, three being evidently the highest among them.

I started along the ridge of my wall, and went to its highest part, that to the S.W., intending to see what I could of the view towards the sea, and then to choose a place for camping in for the night.

When I reached the S.W. end, looking westwards I saw the South Atlantic down below, like a plain of frosted silver. Out of it, barely twenty miles away, rose Fernando Po to its 10,190 feet with that majestic grace peculiar to a volcanic island. Immediately below me, some 10,000 feet or so, lay Victoria with the forested foot-hills of Mungo Mah Lobeh encircling it as a diadem, and Ambas Bay gemmed with rocky islands lying before it. On my left away S.E. was the glorious stretch of the Cameroon estuary, with a line of white cloud lying very neatly along the course of the Cameroon River.

In one of the chasms of the mountain wall that I had come up – in the one furthest to the north – there was a thunderstorm brewing, seemingly hanging on to, or streaming out of the mountain side, a soft billowy mass of dense cream-coloured cloud, with flashes of golden lightnings playing about in it with soft growls of thunder. Surely Mungo Mah Lobeh himself, of all the thousands he annually turns out, never made one more lovely than this. Soon the white mists rose from the mangrove-swamp, and grew rose-colour in the light of the setting sun, as they swept upwards over the now purple high forests. In the heavens, to the north, there was a rainbow, vivid in colour, one arch of it going behind the peak, the other sinking into the mist sea below, and this mist sea rose and rose towards me, turning from pale rose-colour to lavender, and where the shadow of the Mungo lay across it, to a dull leaden grey. It was soon at my feet, blotting the underworld out, and soon came flowing over the wall top at its lowest parts, stretching in great spreading rivers over the crater plain, and then these coalescing everything was shut out save the two summits: that of Cameroon close to me, and that of Clarence away on Fernando Po. These two stood out alone, like great island masses made of iron rising from a formless, silken sea.

The space around seemed boundless, and there was

in it neither sound nor colour, nor anything with form, save those two terrific things. It was like a vision, and it held me spellbound, as I stood shivering on the rocks with the white mist round my knees until into my wool-gathering mind came the memory of those anything but sublime men of mine; and I turned and scuttled off along the rocks like an agitated ant left alone in a dead universe.

I soon found the place where I had come up into the crater plain and went down over the wall, descending with twice the rapidity, but ten times the scratches and grazes, of the ascent.

I picked up the place where I had left Xenia, but no Xenia was there, nor came there any answer to my bush call for him, so on I went down towards the place where, hours ago, I had left the men. The mist was denser down below, but to my joy it was warmer than on the summit of the wind-swept wall.

I had nearly reached the foot of this wall and made my mind up to turn in for the night under a rock, when I heard a melancholy croak away in the mist to the left. I went towards it and found Xenia lost on his own account, and distinctly quaint in manner, and then I recollected that I had been warned Xenia is slightly crazy. Nice situation this: a madman on a mountain in the mist. Xenia, I found, had no longer got my black bag, but in its place a lid of a saucepan and an empty lantern. To put it mildly, this is not the sort of outfit the R.G.S. *Hints to Travellers* would recommend for African exploration. Xenia reported that he gave the bag to Black boy, who shortly afterwards disappeared, and that he had neither seen him nor any of the others since, and didn't expect to this side of Srahmandazi. In a homicidal state of mind, I made tracks for the missing ones followed by Xenia. I thought mayhap they had grown on to the rocks they had sat upon so long, but presently, just before it became quite dark, we picked up the place we had left them in and found there only an empty soda-water bottle. Xenia poured out a muddled mass of observations to the effect that 'they got fright too much about them water palaver.'

I did not linger to raise a monument to them, but I said I wished they were in a condition to require one, and we went on over our hillocks with more confidence now that we knew we had stuck well to our unmarked track.

> 'The moving Moon went up the sky,
>   And nowhere did abide:
> Softly she was going up,
>   And a star or two beside.'

Only she was a young and inefficient moon, and although we were below the thickest of the mist band, it was dark.

Finding our own particular hole in the forest wall was about as easy as finding 'our particular rabbit hole in an unknown hay-field in the dark,' and the attempt to do so afforded us a great deal of varied exercise. I am obliged to be guarded in my language, because my feelings now are only down to one degree below boiling point. The rain now began to fall, thank goodness, and

I drew the thick ears of grass through my parched lips as I stumbled along over the rugged lumps of rock hidden under the now waist-high jungle grass.

Our camp hole was pretty easily distinguishable by daylight, for it was on the left-hand side of one of the forest tongues, the grass land running down like a lane between two tongues here, and just over the entrance three conspicuously high trees showed. But we could not see these 'picking-up' points in the darkness, so I had to keep getting Xenia to strike matches, and hold them in his hat while I looked at the compass. Presently we came full tilt up against a belt of trees which I knew from these compass observations was our tongue of forest belt, and I fired a couple of revolver shots into it, whereabouts I judged our camp to be.

This was instantly answered by a yell from human voices in chorus, and towards that yell in a slightly amiable – a very slightly amiable – state of mind I went.

I will draw a veil over the scene, particularly over my observations to those men. They did not attempt to deny their desertion, but they attempted to explain it, each one saying that it was not he but the other boy who 'got fright too much.'

As the black sergeant was nominally our guide, I asked him for his views on the situation. He said that when he got back to the camp the boys were drunk, which I daresay was true, but left the explanation of why he went back out of the affair. I pointed this out, and Bum, the Head man, charged into the gap with the statement that Black boy had got 'sick in him tummick, he done got fever bad bad too much,' and so he and the rest had to escort Black boy back to camp. This statement, though a contribution to the knowledge of the reason of the return, was manifestly untrue; because Black boy, who did not know English, sat laughing and talking at the fire during this moving recital of his woes. Those men should have rehearsed their explanations, and then Black boy could have done a good rousing writhe to support poor Bum's statement.

I closed the palaver promptly with a brief but lurid sketch of my opinion on the situation, and ordered food, for not having had a thing save that cup of sour claret since 6.30 A.M., and it being now 11 P.M., I felt sinkings. Then arose another beautiful situation before me. It seems when Cook and Monrovia got back into camp this morning Master Cook was seized with one of those attacks of a desire to manage things that produce such awful results in the African servant, and sent all the beef and rice down to Buea to be cooked, because there was no water here to cook it. Therefore the men have got nothing to eat. I had a few tins of my own food and so gave them some, and they became as happy as kings in a few minutes, listening and shouting over the terrible adventures of Xenia, who is posing as the Hero of the Great Cameroon. I get some soda-water from the two bottles left and some tinned herring, and then write out two notes to Herr Liebert asking him to send me three more demijohns of water, and some beef and rice from the store, promising faithfully to pay for them on my return.

I would not prevent those men of mine from going up that peak above me after their touching conduct to-day. Oh! no; not for worlds, dear things.

iii. The Crater

September 24th. – Lovely morning, the grey-white mist in the forest makes it like a dream of Fairyland, each moss-grown tree stem heavily gemmed with dewdrops. At 5.30 I stir the boys, for Sasu, the sergeant, says he must go back to his military duties. The men think we are all going back with him as he is our only guide, but I send three of them down with orders to go back to Victoria – two being of the original set I started with. They are surprised and disgusted at being sent home, but they have got 'hot foot,' and something wrong in the usual seat of African internal disturbances, their 'tummicks,' and I am not thinking of starting a sanatorium for abdominally-afflicted Africans in that crater plain above. Black boy is the other boy returned, I do not want another of his attacks.

They go, and this leaves me in the forest camp with Kefalla, Xenia, and Cook, and we start expecting the water sent for by Monrovia boy yesterday forenoon. There are an abominable lot of bees about; they do not give one a moment's peace, getting beneath the waterproof sheets over the bed, and pretending they can't get out and forthwith losing their tempers, which is imbecile, because the whole four sides of the affair are broad open.

The ground, bestrewn with leaves and dried wood, is a mass of large flies rather like our common house-fly, but both butterflies and beetles seem scarce; but

I confess I do not feel up to hunting much after yesterday's work, and deem it advisable to rest.

My face and particularly my lips are a misery to me, having been blistered all over by yesterday's sun, and last night I inadvertently whipped the skin all off one cheek with the blanket, and it keeps on bleeding, and, horror of horrors, there is no tea until that water comes.

I wish I had got the mountaineering spirit, for then I could say, 'I'll never come to this sort of place again, for you can get all you want in the Alps.' I have been told this by my mountaineering friends – I have never been there – and that you can go and do all sorts of stupendous things all day, and come back in the evening to *table d'hôte* at an hotel; but as I have not got the mountaineering spirit, I suppose I shall come fooling into some such place as this as soon as I get the next chance.

About 8.30, to our delight, the gallant Monrovia boy comes through the bush with a demijohn of water, and I get my tea, and give the men the only half-pound of rice I have and a tin of meat, and they eat, become merry, and chat over their absent companions in a scornful, scandalous way. Who cares for hotels now? When one is in a delightful place like this, one must work, so off I go to the north into the forest, after giving the rest of the demijohn of water into the Monrovia boy's charge with strict orders it is not to be opened till my return. Quantities of beetles.

A little after two o'clock I return to camp, after having wandered about in the forest and found three very deep holes, down which I heaved rocks and in no case heard a splash. In one I did not hear the rocks strike, owing to the great depth. I hate holes, and especially do I hate these African ones, for I am frequently falling, more or less, into them, and they will be my end. So far I have never fallen down a West Coast native gold mine, but I know people who have; but all the other sorts I have tried, having pitched by day and night into those, from three to twelve feet deep, made by industrious indigenous ones, as Mrs Gault calls them, digging out sand and earth to make the 'swish' walls of their simple savage homes; and also into those from twenty to thirty feet deep with pointed stakes at the bottom, artfully disposed to impale the elephant and leopard of the South-West Coast. But my worst fall was into a disused Portuguese well of unknown depth at Cabinda. I 'feel the place in frosty weather still,' though I did not go down all the way, my descent being arrested by a collection of brushwood and rubbish, which had been cast into it, and which had hitched far down in the shaft. When I struck this subterranean wood raft, I thought – Saved! The next minute it struck me that raft was sinking, and so it was, slowly and jerkily, but sinking all the same. I clapper-clawed round in the stuffy dark for something at the side to hang on to, and got some tough bush rope, just as I was convinced that my fate was an inglorious and inverted case of Elijah, and I was being carried off, alive, to Shiöl.

The other demijohns of water have not arrived yet, and we are getting anxious again because the men's food has not come up, and they have been so exceedingly thirsty that they have drunk most of the water – not, however, since it has been in Monrovia's charge; but at 3.15 another boy comes through the bush with another demijohn of water. We receive him gladly, and ask him about the chop. He knows nothing about it. At 3.45 another boy comes through the bush with another demijohn of water; we receive him kindly; *he* does not know anything about the chop. At 4.10 another boy comes through the bush with another demijohn of water, and knowing nothing about the chop, we are civil to him, and that's all.

A terrific tornado which has been lurking growling about then sits down in the forest and bursts, wrapping us up in a lively kind of fog, with its thunder, lightning, and rain. It was impossible to hear, or make one's self heard at the distance of even a few paces, because of the shrill squeal of the wind, the roar of the thunder, and the rush of the rain on the trees round us. It was not like having a storm burst over you in the least; you felt you were in the middle of its engine-room when it had broken down badly. After half an hour or so the thunder seemed to lift itself off the ground, and the lightning came in sheets, instead of in great forks that flew like flights of spears among the forest trees. The thunder, however, had not settled things amicably with the mountain; it roared its rage at Mungo, and Mungo answered back, quivering with a rage as great, under our feet. One feels here as if one were constantly dropping, unasked and unregarded, among painful and violent discussions between the elemental powers of the universe. Mungo growls and swears in thunder at the sky, and sulks in white mist all the morning, and then the sky answers back, hurling down lightnings and rivers of water, with total disregard of Mungo's visitors. The way the water rushes down from the mountain wall through the watercourses in the jungle just above, and then at the edge of the forest spreads out into a sheet of water that is an inch deep, and that flies on past us in miniature cascades, trying the while to put out our fire, and so on, is – quite interesting. (I exhausted my vocabulary on those boys yesterday.)

As soon as we saw what we were in for, we had thrown dry wood on to the fire, and it blazed just as the rain came down, so with our assistance it fought a good fight with its fellow elements, spitting and hissing like a wild cat. It could have managed the water fairly well, but the wind came, very nearly putting an end to it by carrying away its protecting bough house, which settled on 'Professor' Kefalla, who burst out in a lecture on the foolishness of mountaineering and the quantity of devils in this region. Just in the midst of these joys another boy came through the bush with another demijohn of water. We did not receive him even civilly; I burst out laughing, and the boys went off in a roar, and we shouted at him, 'Where them chop?' 'He live for come,' said the boy, and we then gave him a hearty welcome and a tot of rum, and an hour afterwards two more boys appear, one carrying a sack of rice and beef for the men, and the other a box for me from Herr Liebert, containing a luxurious supply of biscuits, candles, tinned meats, and a bottle of wine and one of beer.

We are now all happy, though exceedingly damp, and the boys sit round the fire, with their big iron pot full of beef and rice, busy cooking while they talk. Wonderful accounts of our prodigies of valour I hear given by Xenia, and terrible accounts of what they have lived through from the others, and the men who have brought up the demijohns and the chop recount the last news from Buea. James's wife has run away again.

I have taken possession of two demijohns of water and the rum demijohn, arranging them round the head of my bed. The worst of it is those tiresome bees, as soon as the rain is over, come in hundreds after the rum, and frighten me continually. The worthless wretches get intoxicated on what they can suck from round the cork, and then they stagger about on the ground buzzing malevolently. When the boys have had the chop and a good smoke, we turn to and make up the loads for tomorrow's start up the mountain, and then, after more hot tea, I turn in on my camp bed – listening to the soft sweet murmur of the trees and the pleasant, laughing chatter of the men.

September 25th. – Rolled off the bed twice last night into the bush. The rain has washed the ground away from under its off legs, so that it tilts; and there were quantities of large longicorn beetles about during the night – the sort with spiny backs; they kept on getting themselves hitched on to my blankets and when I wanted civilly to remove them they made a horrid fizzing noise and showed fight – cocking their horns in a defiant way. I awake finally about 5 a.m. soaked through to the skin. The waterproof sheet has had a label sewn to it, so is not waterproof, and it has been raining softly but amply for hours. I wish the camp bed had had a ticket sewn on, and nothing but my profound admiration for Kaiser Wilhelm, Emperor of Germany, its owner, prevents me from making holes in it, for it sags in the middle, and constitutes an excellent rain-water cistern. I have been saying things to it, during the night, about this habit, but the bed is so imbued with the military spirit that it says, 'My orders are to be waterproof, and waterproof I'll be': so I decide to leave it behind, carefully drying it and protecting it as much as possible.

About seven we are off again, with Xenia, head man, cook, Monrovia boy and a labourer from Buea – the water-carriers have gone home after having had their morning chop.

We make for the face of the wall by a route to the left of that I took on Monday, and when we are clambering up it some 600 feet above the hillocks, swish comes a terrific rainstorm at us accompanied by a squealing, bitter cold wind. We can hear the roar of the rain on the forest below, and hoping to get above it we keep on; hoping, however, is vain. The dense mist that comes with it prevents our seeing more than two yards in front, and we get too far to the left. I am behind the band to-day, severely bringing up the rear, and about 1 o'clock I hear shouts from the vanguard and when I get up to them I find them sitting on the edge of one of the clefts or scars in the mountain face.

I do not know how these quarry-like chasms have been formed. They both look alike from below – the mountain wall comes down vertically into them – and the bottom of this one slopes forward, so that if we had had the misfortune when a little lower down to have gone a little further to the left, we should have got on to the bottom of it, and should have found ourselves walled in on three sides, and had to retrace our steps; as it is we have just struck its right-hand edge. And fortunately, the mist, thick as it is, has not been sufficiently thick to lead the men to walk over it; for had they done so they would have got killed, as the cliff arches in under so that we look straight into the bottom of the scar some 200 or 300 feet below, when there is a split in the mist. The sides and bottom are made of, and strewn with, white, moss-grown masses of volcanic cinder rock, and sparsely shrubbed with gnarled trees which have evidently been under fire – one of my boys tells me from the burning of this face of the mountain by 'the Major from Calabar' during the previous dry season.

We keep on up a steep grass-covered slope, and finally reach the top of the wall. The immense old crater floor before us is to-day the site of a seething storm, and the peak itself quite invisible. My boys are quite demoralised by the cold. I find most of them have sold the blankets I gave them out at Buana; and those who have not sold them have left them behind at Buea, from laziness perhaps, but more possibly from a confidence in their powers to prevent us getting so far.

I believe if I had collapsed too – the cold tempted me to do so as nothing else can – they would have lain down and died in the cold sleety rain.

I sight a clump of gnarled sparsely-foliaged trees bedraped heavily with lichen, growing in a hollow among the rocks; thither I urge the men for shelter and they go like storm-bewildered sheep. My bones are shaking in my skin and my teeth in my head, for after the experience I had had of the heat here on Monday I dared not clothe myself heavily.

The men stand helpless under the trees, and I hastily take the load of blankets Herr Liebert lent us off a boy's back and undo it, throwing one blanket round each man, and opening my umbrella and spreading it over the other blankets. Then I give them a tot of rum apiece, as they sit huddled in their blankets, and tear up a lot of the brittle, rotten wood from the trees and shrubs, getting horrid thorns into my hands the while, and set to work getting a fire with it and the driest of the moss from beneath the rocks. By the aid of it and Xenia, who soon revived, and a carefully scraped up candle and a box of matches, the fire soon blazes, Xenia holding a blanket to shelter it, while I, with a cutlass, chop stakes to fix the blankets on, so as to make a fire tent.

The other boys now revive, and I hustle them about to make more fires, no easy work in the drenching rain, but work that has got to be done. We soon get three well alight, and then I clutch a blanket – a wringing wet blanket, but a comfort – and wrapping myself round in it, issue orders for wood to be gathered and stored round each fire to dry, and then stand over cook while he makes the men's already cooked chop hot over our first fire, when this is done getting him to make me tea, or as it more truly should be called, soup, for it contains bits of rice and beef, and the general taste of the affair is wood smoke.

Kefalla by this time is in lecturing form again, so my mind is relieved about him, although he says, 'Oh ma! It be cold, cold too much. Too much cold kill we black man, all same for one as too much sun kill you white man. Oh ma! . . .,' &c. I tell him they have only got themselves to blame; if they had come up with me on Monday we should have been hot enough, and missed this storm of rain.

When the boys have had their chop, and are curling themselves up comfortably round their now blazing fires, Xenia must needs start a theory that there is a better place than this to camp in; he saw it when he was with an unsuccessful expedition that got as far as this. Kefalla is fool enough to go off with him to find this place; but they soon return, chilled through again, and unsuccessful in their quest. I gather that they have been to find caves. I wish they had found caves, for I am not thinking of taking out a patent for our present camp site.

The bitter wind and swishing rain keep on. We are to a certain extent sheltered from the former, but the latter is of that insinuating sort that nothing but a granite wall would keep off.

Just at sundown, however, as is usual in this country, the rain ceases for a while, and I take this opportunity to get out my seaman's jersey, and retire up over the rocks to have my fight into it unobserved. It is a mighty fight to get that thing on, or off, at the best of times, but to-day it is worse than usual, because I have to get it on over my saturated cotton blouse, and verily at one time I fear I shall have to shout for assistance or be suffocated, so firmly does it get jammed over my head. But I fight my way unaided into it, and then turn to survey our position, and find I have been carrying on my battle on the brink of an abysmal hole whose mouth is concealed among the rocks and scraggly shrubs just above our camp. I heave rocks down it, as we in Fanland would offer rocks to an Ombwiri, and hear them go 'knickity-knock, like a pebble in Carisbrook well.' I think I detect a far away splash, but it was an awesome way down. This mountain seems set with these man-traps, and 'some day some gentleman's nigger' will get killed down one.

The mist has now cleared away from the peak, but lies all over the lower world, and I take bearings of the three highest cones or peaks carefully. Then I go away over the rocky ground southwards, and as I stand look-ing round, the mist sea below is cleft in twain for a few minutes by some fierce down-draught of wind from the peak, and I get a strange, clear, sudden view right down to Ambas Bay. It is just like looking down from one world into another. I think how Odin hung and looked down into Nifelheim, and then of how hot, how deliciously hot, it was away down there, and then the mist closes over it. I shiver and go back to camp, for night is coming on, and I know my men will require intellectual support in the matter of procuring firewood.

The men are now quite happy; over each fire they

have made a tent with four sticks with a blanket on, a blanket that is too wet to burn, though I have to make them brace the blankets to windward for fear of their scorching.

The wood from the shrubs here is of an aromatic and a resinous nature, which sounds nice, but it isn't; for the volumes of smoke it gives off when burning are suffocating, and the boys, who sit almost on the fire, are every few moments scrambling to their feet and going apart to cough out smoke, like so many novices in training for the profession of fire-eaters. However, they soon find that if they roll themselves in their blankets, and lie on the ground to windward they escape most of the smoke. They have divided up into three parties: Kefalla and Xenia, who have struck up a great friendship, take the lower, the most exposed fire. Head man, Cook, and Monrovia Boy have the upper fire, and the labourer has the middle one – he being an outcast for medical reasons. They are all steaming away and smoking comfortably.

I form the noble resolution to keep awake, and rouse up any gentleman who may catch on fire during the night, a catastrophe which is inevitable, and see to wood being put on the fires, so elaborately settle myself on my wooden chop-box, wherein I have got all the lucifers which are not in the soap-box. The very address on that chop-box ought to keep its inside dry and up to duty, for it is 'An den Hochwohlgebornen Freiherrn von Stettin,' &c. Owing to there not being a piece of ground the size of a sixpenny piece level in this place, the arrangement of my box camp takes time, but at last it is done to my complete satisfaction, close to a tree trunk, and I think, as I wrap myself up in my two wet blankets and lean against my tree, what a good thing it is to know how to make one's self comfortable in a place like this. This tree stem is perfection, just the right angle to be restful to one's back, and one can rely all the time on Nature hereabouts not to let one get thoroughly effete from luxurious comfort, so I lazily watch and listen to Xenia and Kefalla at their fire hard by.

They commence talking to each other on their different tribal societies; Kefalla is a Very, Xenia a Liberian, so in the interests of science I give them two heads of tobacco to stimulate their conversation. They receive them with tragic grief, having no pipe, so in the interests of science I undo my blankets and give them two out of my portmanteau; then do myself up again and pretend to be asleep. I am rewarded by getting some interesting details, and form the opinion that both these worthies, in their pursuit of their particular ju-jus, have come into contact with white prejudices, and are now fugitives from religious persecution. I also observe they have both their own ideas of happiness. Kefalla holds it lies in a warm shirt; Xenia that it abides in warm trousers; and every half-hour the former takes his shirt off, and holds it in the fire smoke, and then puts it hastily on; and Xenia, who is the one and only trouser wearer in our band, spends fifty per cent of the night on one leg struggling to get the other in or out of these garments, when they are either coming off to be warmed, or going on after warming. Those trousers of Xenia's have something wrong about them; I don't pretend to understand the garment, never having gone in for that sort of thing myself, but it is my belief he slings them too high, with those braces, which *more Alemanni* he wears. Anyhow, in season and out, they want taking off. Three mortal times to-day when on that wind- and rain-swept wall, the whole of us have been brought to a standstill by Xenia having to stand on one leg and do something to his peculiar vestments. It's a mercy he did not kill himself when he fell over while engaged in these operations among the rocks this afternoon – as it is, I see he has smashed the lantern glass again, so that I have to keep it under my blankets to prevent the candle getting blown out by this everlasting N.E. wind.

There seem but few insects here. I have only got two moths to-night – one pretty one with white wings with little red spots on, like an old-fashioned petticoat such as an early Victorian-age lady would have worn – the other a sweet thing in silver.

Then a horrid smell of burning negro interrupts my writing and I have to get up and hunt it down. After some trouble I find it is a spark in cook's hair, he sleeping the while sweetly. I rouse him, via his shins, and tell him to put himself out, and he is grateful.

My face is a misery to me, as soon as it dries it sets into a mask, and when I move it, it splits and bleeds.

(Later, *i.e.*, 2.15 A.M.). I have been asleep against that abominable vegetable of a tree. It had its trunk covered with a soft cushion of moss, and pretended to be a comfort – a right angle to lean against, and a softly padded protection to the spine from wind, and all that sort of thing; whereas the whole mortal time it was nothing in this wretched world but a water-pipe, to conduct an extra supply of water down my back. The water has simply streamed down it, and formed a nice little pool in a rocky hollow where I keep my feet, and I am chilled to the innermost bone, so have to scramble up and drag my box to the side of Kefalla and Xenia's fire, feeling sure I have contracted a fatal chill this time. I scrape the ashes out of the fire into a heap, and put my sodden boots into them, and they hiss merrily, and I resolve not to go to sleep again.

5 A.M. – Have been to sleep twice, and have fallen off my box bodily into the fire in my wet blankets, and should for sure have put it out like a bucket of cold water had not Xenia and Kefalla been roused up by the smother I occasioned and rescued me – or the fire. It is not raining now, but it is bitter cold and cook is getting my tea. I give the boys a lot of hot tea with a big handful of sugar in, and they then get their own food hot.

iv. *The Summit*

September 26th. – The weather is undecided and so am I for I feel doubtful about going on in this weather, but I do not like to give up the peak after going through so much for it. The boys being dry and warm with the fires have forgotten their troubles. However, I settle in my mind to keep on, and ask for volunteers to come with me, and Bum, the head man, and Xenia announce their willingness. I put two tins of meat and a bottle of Herr Liebert's beer into the little wooden box, and insist on both men taking a blanket apiece, much to their disgust, and before six o'clock we are off over the crater plain. It is a broken bit of country with rock mounds sparsely overgrown with tufts of grass, and here and there are patches of boggy land, not real bog, but damp places where grow little clumps of rushes, and here and there among the rocks sorely-afflicted shrubs of broom, and the yellow-flowered shrub I have mentioned before, and quantities of very sticky heather, feeling when you catch hold of it as if it had been covered with syrup. One might fancy the entire race of shrubs was dying out; for one you see partially alive there are twenty skeletons which fall to pieces as you brush past them.

It is downhill the first part of the way, that is to say, the trend of the land is downhill, for be it down or up, the details of it are rugged mounds and masses of burnt-out lava rock. It is evil going, but perhaps not quite so evil as the lower hillocks of the great wall where the rocks are hidden beneath long slippery grass. We wind our way in between the mounds, or clamber over them, or scramble along their sides impartially. The general level is then flat, and then comes a rise towards the peak wall, so we steer N.N.E. until we strike the face of the peak, and then commence a stiff rough climb. We are all short of breath, but I do not think from the altitude; my shortness arises from a cold I have got, and my men's from too much breakfast, I fancy.

We keep as straight as we can, but get driven at an angle by the strange ribs of rock which come straight down. These are most tiresome to deal with, getting worse the higher we go, and so rotten and weather-eaten are they that they crumble into dust and fragments under our feet. Head man gets half a dozen falls, and when we are about three parts of the way up Xenia gives in. The cold and the climbing are too much for him, so I make him wrap himself up in his blanket, which he is glad enough of now, and shelter in a depression under one of the many rock ridges, and head man and I go on. When we are some 600 feet higher the iron-grey mist comes curling and waving round the rocks above us, like some savage monster defending them from intruders, and I again debate whether I was justified in risking the men, for it is a risk for them at this low temperature, with the evil weather I know, and they do not know, is coming on. But still we have food and blankets with us enough for them, and the camp in the plain below they can reach all right, if the worst comes to the worst; and for myself

– well – that's my own affair, and no one will be a ha'porth the worse if I am dead in an hour. So I hitch myself on to the rocks, and take bearings, particularly bearings of Xenia's position, who, I should say, has got a tin of meat and a flask of rum with him, and then turn and face the threatening mist. It rises and falls, and sends out arm-like streams towards us, and then Bum, the head man, decides to fail for the third time to reach the peak, and I leave him wrapped in his blanket with the bag of provisions, and go on alone into the wild, grey, shifting, whirling mist above, and soon find myself at the head of a rock ridge in a narrowish depression, walled by massive black walls which show fitfully but firmly through the mist.

I can see three distinctly high cones before me, and then the mist, finding it cannot drive me back easily, proceeds to desperate methods, and lashes out with a burst of bitter wind, and a sheet of blinding, stinging rain. I make my way up through it towards a peak which I soon see through a tear in the mist is not the highest, so I angle off and go up the one to the left, and after a desperate fight reach the cairn – only, alas! to find a hurricane raging and a fog in full possession, and not a ten yards' view to be had in any direction. Near the cairn on the ground are several bottles, some of which the energetic German officers, I suppose, had emptied in honour of their achievement, an achievement I bow down before, for their pluck and strength had taken them here in a shorter time by far than mine. I do not meddle with anything, save to take a few specimens and to put a few more rocks on the cairn, and to put in among them my card, merely as a civility to Mungo, a civility his Majesty will soon turn into pulp. Not that it matters – what is done is done.

The weather grows worse every minute, and no sign of any clearing shows in the indigo sky or the wind-reft mist. The rain lashes so fiercely I cannot turn my face to it and breathe, the wind is all I can do to stand up against.

Verily I am no mountaineer, for there is in me no exultation, but only a deep disgust because the weather has robbed me of my main object in coming here, namely to get a good view and an idea of the way the unexplored mountain range behind Calabar trends.

No doubt had the weather been clear I should have been able to do this well, for the whole Omon range must be visible from this great summit of Cameroons, which rises at right angles to it. For when I was in Okyon close to this Rumby or Omon range, Mungo's great mass was perfectly visible looking seawards. My only consolation is that my failure to do this bit of work is not my own fault, save as regards my coming here at the wrong season, which matter was also beyond my control. Moreover there was just the chance, as this is the tornado season, and not the real wet, that I might have had a clear day on the peak. I took my chance and it failed, so there's nothing to complain about.

Comforting myself with these reflections, I start down to find Bum, and do so neatly, and then together we scramble down carefully among the rotten black rocks, intent on finding Xenia. The scene is very grand. At one minute we can see nothing save the black rocks and cinders under foot; the next the wind-torn mist separates now in one direction, now in another, showing us always the same wild scene of great black cliffs, rising in jagged peaks and walls around and above us. I think this walled cauldron we had just left is really the highest crater on Mungo.

We soon become anxious about Xenia, for this is a fearfully easy place to lose a man in such weather, but just as we get below the thickest part of the pall of mist, I observe a doll-sized figure, standing on one leg taking on or off its trousers – our lost Xenia, beyond a shadow of a doubt, and we go down direct to him.

When we reach him we halt, and I give the two men one of the tins of meat, and take another and the bottle of beer myself, and then make a hasty sketch of the great crater plain below us. At the further edge of the plain a great white cloud is coming up from below, which argues badly for our trip down the great wall to the forest camp, which I am anxious to reach before nightfall after our experience of the accommodation afforded by our camp in the crater plain last night.

While I am sitting waiting for the men to finish their meal, I feel a chill at my back, as if some cold thing had settled there, and turning round, see the mist from the summit above coming in a wall down towards us. These mists up here, as far as my experience goes, are always preceded by a strange breath of ice-cold air – not necessarily a wind.

Bum then draws my attention to a strange funnel-shaped thing coming down from the clouds to the north. A big waterspout, I presume: it seems to be moving rapidly N.E., and I profoundly hope it will hold that course, for we have quite as much as we can manage with the ordinary rain-water supply on this mountain, without having waterspouts to deal with.

We start off down the mountain as rapidly as we can. Xenia is very done up, and Head man comes perilously near breaking his neck by frequent falls among the rocks; my unlucky boots are cut through and through by the latter. When we get down towards the big crater plain, it is a race between us and the pursuing mist as to who shall reach the camp first, and the mist wins, but we have just time to make out the camp's exact position before it closes round us, so we reach it without any real difficulty. When we get there, about one o'clock, I find the men have kept the fires alight and Cook is asleep before one of them with another conflagration smouldering in his hair. I get him to make me tea, while the others pack up as quickly as possible, and by two we are all off on our way down to the forest camp.

The boys are nervous in their way of going down over the mountain wall. The misadventures of Cook alone would fill volumes. Monrovia boy is out and away the best man at this work. Just as we reach the high jungle grass, down comes the rain and up comes the mist, and we have the worst time we have had during our whole trip, in our endeavours to find the hole in the forest that leads to our old camp.

Unfortunately, I must needs go in for acrobatic performances on the top of one of the highest, rockiest hillocks. Poising myself on one leg I take a rapid slide sideways, ending in a very showy leap backwards which lands me on the top of the lantern I am carrying to-day, among miscellaneous rocks. There being fifteen feet or so of jungle grass above me, all the dash and beauty of my performance are as much thrown away as I am, for my boys are too busy on their own accounts in the mist to miss me. After resting some little time as I fell, and making and unmaking the idea in my mind that I am killed, I get up, clamber elaborately to the top of the next hillock, and shout for the boys, and 'Ma,' 'Ma,' comes back from my flock from various points out of the fog. I find Bum and Monrovia boy, and learn that during my absence Xenia, who always fancies himself as a path-finder, has taken the lead, and gone off somewhere with the rest. We shout and the others answer, and we join them, and it soon becomes evident to the meanest intelligence that Xenia had better have spent his time attending to those things of his instead of going in for guiding, for we are now right off the track we made through the grass on our up journey, and we proceed to have a cheerful hour or so in the wet jungle, ploughing hither and thither, trying to find our way.

At last we pick up the top of a tongue of forest that we all feel is ours, but we – that is to say, Xenia and I, for the others go like lambs to the slaughter wherever they are led – disagree as to the path. He wants to go down one side of the tongue, I to go down the other, and I have my way, and we wade along, skirting the bushes that fringe it, trying to find our hole. I own I soon begin to feel shaky about having been right in the affair, but soon Xenia, who is leading, shouts he has got it, and we limp in, our feet sore with rugged rocks, and everything we have on, or in the loads, wringing wet, save the matches, which providentially I had put into my soap-box.

Anything more dismal than the look of that desired camp when we reach it, I never saw. Pools of water everywhere. The fire-house a limp ruin, the camp bed I have been thinking fondly of for the past hour a water cistern. I tilt the water out of it, and say a few words to it regarding its hide-bound idiocy in obeying its military instructions to be waterproof; and then, while the others are putting up the fire-house, head man and I get out the hidden demijohn of rum, and the beef and rice, and I serve out a tot of rum each to the boys, who are shivering dreadfully, waiting for cook to get the fire. He soon does this, and then I have my hot tea and the men their hot food, for now we have returned to the luxury of two cooking pots.

Their education in bush is evidently progressing, for they make themselves a big screen with boughs and spare blankets, between the wind and the fire-house, and I get Xenia to cut some branches, and place them on the top of my waterproof sheet shelter, and we are fairly comfortable again, and the boys quite merry and very well satisfied with themselves.

Unfortunately the subject of their nightly debating society is human conduct, a subject ever fraught with dangerous elements of differences of opinion. They are busy discussing, with their mouths full of rice and beef, the conduct of an absent friend, who it seems is generally regarded by them as a spendthrift. 'He gets plenty money, but he no have none no time.' 'He go frow it away on woman, and drink.' 'He no buy clothes.' This last is evidently a very heavy accusation, but Kefalla says, 'What can a man buy with money better than them thing he like best?'

This philosophic outburst from Kefalla is followed by a wordy war on the innate worthlessness of woman and drink, the details of which I will not give, but presently there is an extra row, and Cook rushes to me, holding in one hand the cooking pot, into which I find I am expected to shove my nose, and then to sniff at his abominably dirty singlet. Kefalla comes hurrying after him talking sixteen to the dozen. It seems that during the discussion of a particularly knotty point on practical ethics, Kefalla fell out with Cook, and seizing his rum and water, threw it at him, and what has not gone over Cook has gone into his supper in the pot. Cook displays a lively horror of the smell of rum in his rice, which is, coming from him, a bit comic. I call up head man, who is as usual not attending to his duty of keeping the others in order, and we two talk the palaver and decide, in spite of Kefalla's specious arguments, that he is to pay Cook for both the rice and the rum, and the latter goes off content, vowing he'll have their value to the last farthing out of Kefalla. The men then gradually go off to sleep, breaking out now and again spasmodically into little rows over a pipe, and so on, until at last all is peace.

There is a very peculiar look on the rotten wood on the ground round here; to-night it has patches and flecks of iridescence like one sees on herrings or mackerel that have been kept too long. The appearance of this strange eerie light in among the bush is very weird and charming. I have seen it before in dark forests at night, but never so much of it.

September 27th. – Fine morning. It's a blessing my Pappenheimers have not recognised what this means for the afternoon. We take things very leisurely. I know it's no good hurrying, we are dead sure of getting a ducking before we reach Buea anyhow, so we may as well enjoy ourselves while we can.

I ask my boys how they would 'make fire suppose no matches live.' Not one of them thinks it possible to do so, 'it pass man to do them thing suppose he no got live stick or matches.' They are coast boys, all of them, and therefore used to luxury, but it is really remarkable how widely diffused matches are inland, and how very dependent on them these natives are. When I have been away in districts where they have not penetrated, it is exceedingly rarely that the making of fire has to be resorted to. I think I may say that in most African villages it has not had to be done for years and years, because when a woman's fire has gone out, owing to her having been out at work all day, she just runs into some neighbour's hut where there is a fire burning, and gives compliments, and picks up a burning stick from the fire and runs home. From this comes the compliment, equivalent to our 'Oh! don't go away yet,' of 'You come to fetch fire.' This will be said to you all the way from Sierra Leone to Loanda, as far as I know, if you have been making yourself agreeable in an African home, even if the process may have extended over a day or so. The hunters, like the Fans, have to make fire, and do it now with a flint and steel; but in districts where their tutor in this method – the flint-lock gun – is not available, they will do it with two sticks, not always like the American Indians' fire-sticks. One stick is placed horizontally on the ground and the other twirled rapidly between the palms of the hands, but sometimes two bits of palm stick are worked in a hole in a bigger bit of wood, the hole stuffed round with the pith of a tree or with silk or cotton fluff, and the two sticks rotated vigorously. Again, on one occasion I saw a Bakele woman make fire by means of a slip of rafia palm drawn very rapidly, to and fro, across a notch in another piece of rafia wood. In most domesticated tribes, like the Effiks or the Igalwa, if they are going out to their plantation, they will enclose a live stick in a hollow piece of a certain sort of wood, which has a lining of its interior pith left in it, and they will carry this 'fire box' with them. Or if they are going on a long canoe journey, there is always the fire in the bow of the canoe put into a calabash full of sand, or failing that, into a bed of clay with a sand rim round it.

By 10 o'clock we are off down to Buea. At 10.15 it pours as it can here; by 10.17 we are all in our normal condition of bedraggled saturation, and plodding down carefully and cheerfully among the rocks and roots of the forest, following the path we have beaten and cut for ourselves on our way up. It is dangerously slippery, particularly that part of it through the amomums, and stumps of the cut amomums are very likely to spike your legs badly – and, my friend, never, never, step on one of the amomum stems lying straight in front of you, particularly when they are soaking wet. Ice slides are nothing to them, and when you fall, as you inevitably must, because all the things you grab hold of are either rotten, or as brittle as Salviati glass-ware vases, you hurt yourself in no end of places on those aforesaid cut amomum stumps. I am speaking from sad experiences of my own, amplified by observations on the experiences of my men.

The path, when we get down again into the tree-fern region is inches deep in mud and water, and several places where we have a drop of five feet or so over lumps of rock are worse work going down than we found them going up, especially when we have to drop down on to amomum stems. One abominable place, a V-shaped hollow, mud-lined, and with an immense tree right across it – a tree one of our tornadoes has thrown down since we passed – bothers the men badly, as they slip and scramble down, and then crawl under the tree and slip and scramble up with their loads. I say nothing about myself. I just take a flying slide of twenty feet or so and shoot flump under the tree on my back, and then deliberate whether it is worth while getting up again to go on with such a world; but vanity forbids my dying like a dog in a ditch, and I scramble up, rejoining the others where they are standing on a cross-path: our path going S.E. by E., the other S.S.W. Two men have already gone down the S.W. one, which I feel sure is the upper end of the path Sasu had led us to and wasted time on our first day's march; the middle regions of which were, as we had found from its lower end, impassable with vegetation. So after futile attempts to call the other two back, we go on down the S.E. one, and get shortly into a plantation of giant kokos mid-leg deep in most excellent fine mould – the sort of stuff you pay 6s. a load for in England to start a conservatory bed with. Upon my word, the quantities of things there are left loose in Africa, that ought to be kept in menageries and green-houses and not let go wild about the country, are enough to try a saint.

We then pass through a clump of those lovely great tree-ferns. The way their young fronds come up with a graceful curl, like the top of a bishop's staff, is a poem; but being at present fractious, I will observe that they are covered with horrid spines, as most young vegetables are in Africa. But talking about spines, I should remark that nothing save that precious climbing palm – I never like to say what I feel about climbing palms, because one once saved my life – equals the strong bush rope which abounds here. It is covered with short, strong, curved thorns. It creeps along con-cealed by decorative vegetation, and you get your legs twined in it, and of course injured. It festoons itself from tree to tree, and when your mind is set on other things, catches you under the chin, and gives you the appearance of having made a determined but ineffec-tual attempt to cut your throat with a saw. It whisks your hat off and grabs your clothes, and commits other iniquities too numerous to catalogue here. Years and years that bush rope will wait for a man's blood, and when he comes within reach it will have it.

We are well down now among the tree-stems grown over with rich soft green moss and delicate filmy-ferns. I should think that for a botanist these south-eastern slopes of Mungo Mah Lobeh would be the happiest hunting grounds in all West Africa.

The vegetation here is at the point of its supreme luxuriance, owing to the richness of the soil; the leaves of trees and plants I recognise as having seen elsewhere are here far larger, and the undergrowth particularly is more rich and varied, far and away. Ferns seem to find here a veritable paradise. Everything, in fact, is growing at its best. I dare say a friend of mine who told me that near Victoria he had stuck his umbrella into the ground one evening, and found in the morning it was growing leaves all up its stick, was overstating the facts of the case; still, if the incident could happen anywhere it would be in this region.

We come to another fallen tree over another hole; this tree we recognise as an old acquaintance near Buea, and I feel disgusted, for I had put on a clean blouse, and washed my hands in a tea-cupful of water in a cooking pot before leaving the forest camp, so as to look presentable on reaching Buea, and not give Herr Liebert the same trouble he had to recognise the white from the black members of the party that he said he had with the members of the first expedition to the peak; and all I have got to show for my exertion that is clean or anything like dry is one cuff over which I have been carrying a shawl.

We double round a corner by the stockade of the station's plantation, and are at the top of the mud glissade – the new Government path, I should say – that leads down into the barrack-yard.

In the wild exhilaration the view of the barrack-yard and the official residence gives me, I feel mightily inclined to toboggan down it, but I observe what I imagine to be Society on his verandah, and so forbear. But I find when I reach the verandah I might have done it, for Society was superintending making a back drain for surface water and it was only Society's washing that was drying from the wash that had alarmed me.

Our arrival brings Herr Liebert promptly on the scene, as kindly helpful and energetic as ever, and again anxious for me to have a bath. The men bring our saturated loads into my room, and after giving them their food and plenty of tobacco, I get my hot tea and change into the clothes I had left behind at Buea, and feeling once more fit for polite society go out and find his Imperial and Royal Majesty's representative making a door, tightening the boards up with wedges in a very artful and professional way. We discourse on things in general and the mountain in particular. The great south-east face is now showing clear before us, the clearness that usually comes before nightfall. It looks again a vast wall, and I wish I were going up it again to-morrow. When 'the Calabar major' set it on fire in the dry season it must have been a noble sight, and it is small wonder Cameroons thought 'die grosse Kolonie' was going to be Pompeied by an awful eruption from 'der grossen Kolonie am grössten feuerspeienden Berg.'

The north-eastern edge of the slope of the mountain seems to me unbroken up to the peak. The great crater we went and camped in must be a very early one in the history of the mountain, and out of it the present summit seems to have been thrown up. From the sea face, the western, I am told the slope is continuous on the whole, although there are several craters on that side; seventy craters all told are so far known on Mungo.

The last reported eruption was in 1852, when signs of volcanic activity were observed by a captain who was passing at sea. The lava from this eruption must have gone down the western side, for I have come across no fresh lava beds in my wanderings on the other face. Herr Liebert has no confidence in the mountain whatsoever, and announces his intention of leaving Buea with the army on the first symptom of renewed volcanic activity. I attempt to discourage him from this energetic plan, pointing out to him the beauty of that Roman soldier at Pompeii who was found, centuries after that eruption, still at his post; and if he regards that as merely mechanical virtue, why not pursue the plan of the elder Pliny? Herr Liebert planes away at his door, and says it's not in his orders to make scientific observations on volcanoes in a state of eruption. When it is he'll do so – until it is, he most decidedly will not. He adds Pliny was an admiral and sailors are always as curious as cats.

Buea seems a sporting place for weather even without volcanic eruptions, during the whole tornado season (there are two a year), over-charged tornadoes burst in the barrack yard. From the 14th of June till the 27th of August you never see the sun, because of the terrific and continuous wet season downpour. At the beginning and end of this cheerful period occurs a month's tornado season, and the rest of the year is dry, hot by day and cold by night.

They are talking of making Buea into a sanatorium for the fever-stricken. I do not fancy somehow that it's a suitable place for a man who has got all the skin off his nerves with fever and quinine, and is very liable to chill; but all Governments on the Coast, English, German, or French, are stark mad on the subject of sanatoriums in high places, though the experience they have had of them has clearly pointed out that they are valueless in West Africa, and a man's one chance is to get out to sea on a ship that will take him outside the three-mile-deep fever-belt of the coast. I hear grand accounts of other people who have gone up the peak, or tried to; I gather most of the failures have been on account of the porters. Herr Leist went up once from Babundi, and once this side. This side he failed because the three boys he had with him nearly died from the cold, and would have done so entirely if he and Herr Yost, who was with him, had not taken a world of trouble to wrap them in blankets, and rub them, and then, on the boys' account, return down. My Head man, Bum, was with Herr Leist when he tried the sea face side from Babundi and he says they turned back then because it was too steep. I am sure the boys collapsed on that side too, if the truth were known. The only point I congratulate myself on is having got my men up so high, and back again, undamaged; but, as they said, I was a Father and a Mother to them, and a very stern though kind set of parents I have been. I cannot help thinking how very perfectly Kipling's observations on the 'Oont fit the African carrier, for like the commissariat camel

'E's a devil an' an ostrich an' an orphan child in one.

also

'E'll gall and chafe and lame and fight,
'E smells most awful vile,
'E'll lose hisself for ever, if you let him stray a mile.
'E's game to graze the 'ole day long
And 'owl the ole night through;
An' when he comes to greasy ground
He splits hisself in two.

Volumes upon volumes all illustrated with instantaneous photographs, and stiff with statistics, couldn't give you a truer account of him. For instance there are those two who strayed down that other path this afternoon, just coming down the slide in front of us, thank goodness! for I was making up my mind it was my pater-maternal duty to go and find them.

Herr Liebert gives me some interesting details about the first establishment of the station here and a bother he had with the plantations. Only a short time ago the soldiers brought him in some black wood spikes, which they had found with their feet, set into the path leading to the station's koko plantations, to the end of laming the men. On further investigation there were also found pits, carefully concealed with sticks and leaves, and the bottoms lined with bad thorns, also with malicious intent. The local Bakwiri chiefs were called in and asked to explain these phenomena existing in a country where peace had been concluded, and the chiefs said it was quite a mistake, those things had not been put there to kill soldiers, but only to attract their attention, to kill and injure their own fellow-tribesmen who had not been stealing from plantations latterly. That's the West African's way entirely all along the Coast; the 'child-like' native will turn out and shoot you with a gun to attract your attention to the fact that a tribe you never heard of has been and stolen one of his ladies, whom you never saw. It's the sweet infant's way of 'rousing up popular opinion,' but I do not admire or approve of it. If I am to be shot for a crime, for goodness' sake let me commit the crime first.

September 28th. – Down to Victoria in one day, having no desire to renew and amplify my acquaintance with the mission station at Buana. It poured torrentially all the day through. I wonder what it is like here in the wet season; something rather like the climate of the bed of the Atlantic, I presume.

My boots are a dreadful nuisance to-day. I got them dried last night for the first time since I left Victoria, and they are like boards. Xenia brought them to me this morning and I congratulated him on being able to do without boots, but he proudly pointed to his distorted toe-joints, and informed me that once he always wore boots, better boots than mine, and boots that were 'all shiny.' I am sure Xenia has had a chequered past; he is from the Republic of Liberia. I wonder whether he is a fugitive president or a defaulting bank manager? They have copies of all the high points of American culture there, I am told.

The old chief at Buana was very nice to-day when we were coming through his territory. He came out to meet us with some of his wives. Both men and women among these Bakwiri are tattooed, or rather painted, on the body, face and arms, but as far as I have seen not on the legs. The patterns are handsome, and more elaborate than any such that I have seen. One man who came with the party had two figures of men tattooed on the region where his waistcoat should have been. I gave the chief some tobacco though he never begged for anything. He accepted it thankfully, and handing it to his wives preceded us on our path for about a mile and a half and then having reached the end of his district, we shook hands and parted.

After all the rain we have had, the road was of course worse than ever, and as we were going through the forest towards the war hedge, I noticed a strange sound, a dull roar which made the light friable earth quiver under our feet, and I remembered with alarm the accounts Herr Liebert has given me of the strange ways of rivers on this mountain; how by Buea, about 200 metres below where you cross it, the river goes bodily down a hole. How there is a waterfall on the south face of the mountain that falls right into another hole, and is never seen again, any more than the Buea River is. How there are in certain places underground rivers, which though never seen can be heard roaring, and felt in the quivering earth under foot in the wet season, and so on. So I judged our present roar arose from some such phenomenon, and with feminine nervousness began to fear that the rotten water-logged earth we were on might give way, and engulf the whole of us, and we should never be seen again. But when we got down into our next ravine, the one where I got the fish and water-spiders on our way up, things explained themselves. The bed of this ravine was occupied by a raging torrent of great beauty, but alarming appearance to a person desirous of getting across to the other side of it. On our right hand was a waterfall of tons of water thirty feet high or so. The brown water wreathed with foam dashed down into the swirling pool we faced, and at the other edge of the pool, striking a ridge of higher rock, it flew up in a lovely flange some twelve feet or so high, before making another and a deeper spring to form a second waterfall. My men shouted to me above the roar that it was 'a bad place.' They never give me half the credit I deserve for seeing danger, and they said, 'Water all go for hole down there, we fit to go too suppose we fall.' 'Don't fall,' I yelled which was the only good advice I could think of to give them just then.

Each small load had to be carried across by two men along a submerged ridge in the pool, where the water was only breast high. I had all I could do to get through it, though assisted by my invaluable Bakwiri staff. But no harm befell. Indeed we were all the better for it, or at all events cleaner. We met five torrents that had to be waded during the day; none so bad as the first, but all superbly beautiful.

When we turned our faces westwards just above the wood we had to pass through before getting into the great road, the view of Victoria, among its hills, and fronted by its bay, was divinely lovely and glorious with colour. I left the boys here, as they wanted to rest, and to hunt up water, &c., among the little cluster of huts that are here on the right-hand side of the path, and I went on alone down through the wood, and out on to the road, where I found my friend, the Alsatian engineer, still flourishing and busy with his cheery gang of wood-cutters. I made a brief halt here, getting some soda water. I was not anxious to reach Victoria before nightfall, but yet to reach it before dinner, and while I was chatting, my boys came through the wood and the engineer most kindly gave them a tot of brandy apiece, to which I owe their arrival in Victoria. I left them again resting, fearing I had overdone my arrangements for arriving just after nightfall and went on down that road which was more terrible than ever now to my bruised, weary feet, but even more lovely than ever in the dying light of the crimson sunset, with all its dark shadows among the trees begemmed with countless fire-flies – and so safe into Victoria – sneaking up the Government House hill by the private path through the Botanical Gardens.

Idabea, the steward, turned up, and I asked him to let me have some tea and bread and butter, for I was dreadfully hungry. He rushed off, and I heard tremendous operations going on [in] the room above. In a few seconds water poured freely down through the dining-room ceiling. It was bath palaver again. The excellent Idabea evidently thought it was severely wanted, more wanted than such vanities as tea. Fortunately, Herr von Lucke was away down in town, looking after duty as usual, so I was tidy before he returned to dinner. When he returned he had the satisfaction a prophet should feel. I had got half-drowned, and I had got an awful cold, the most awful cold in the head of modern times, I believe, but he was not artistically exultant over my afflictions.

My men having all reported themselves safe I went to my comfortable rooms, but could not turn in, so fascinating was the warmth and beauty down here; and as I sat on the verandah overlooking Victoria and the sea, in the dim soft light of the stars, with the fire-flies round me, and the lights of Victoria away below, and heard the soft rush of the Lukola River, and the sound of the sea-surf on the rocks, and the tom-tomming and singing of the natives, all matching and mingling together, 'Why did I come to Africa?' thought I. Why! who would not come to its twin brother hell itself for all the beauty and the charm of it!